Fitness
and
Figure Control
The Creation
of You

SECOND EDITION

Linda Garrison
Phyllis Leslie
Deborah L. Blackmore

Mt. San Antonio College

 MAYFIELD PUBLISHING COMPANY

Second edition copyright ©1981 by
Mayfield Publishing Company
First edition copyright ©1974 by
Linda Garrison, Phyllis Leslie, and Deborah Blackmore
Second edition 1981

Library of Congress Catalog Card Number: 81-81277
International Standard Book Number: 0-87484-549-1

Manufactured in the United States of America
Mayfield Publishing Company
285 Hamilton Avenue
Palo Alto, California 94301

Compositor: Acme Type Company
Printer and binder: George Banta Company
Sponsoring editor: C. Lansing Hays
Managing editor: Judith Ziajka
Manuscript editor: Phil Cecchettini
Designer: Nancy Sears
Illustrator: Bob Carr
Layout: Mary Wiley
Production: Michelle Hogan
Poem on page 6 from *The Poetry of Robert Frost* edited by
Edward Connery Lathem. Copyright 1916, ©1969 by
Holt, Rinehart, and Winston, Inc. Copyright 1944 by
Robert Frost. Reprinted by permission of Holt,
Rinehart, and Winston, Inc.

Contents

Preface

We believe in life! It is a challenge to exist in today's world, to be sure, but what a wonderful challenge. When there is harmony between mind and body, when we are in touch with ourselves, as individuals, we experience a surge of well-being, freedom and strength, and an awareness of untapped joys and potentials. A zest for living replaces the meaningless humdrum, regardless of our circumstances of home or job. How do we achieve this harmony? One way is through exercise. When we consciously place ourselves in control of the fitness of our bodies, we are taking a first positive step toward shaping our bodies and our lives.

That is why this is more than a book on exercise. The book is designed to help you begin freeing that person deep inside of you. As you follow the exercise program, you will find a new charge of positive energy with which to meet each day. The improvement in your physical being will affect your mental awareness and your creative abilities. Each day will bring you closer to a harmony of body and mind.

In the second edition of *Fitness and Figure Control,* we follow the same basic plan that was so successful in the first edition. The dozens of you who sent in your comments said "we like it as it is," and so we tried to please you. The new edition also offers some additional material that should help you move more surely toward a fit and healthy body. In particular, we now go into much greater detail about the importance of good nutrition and how to achieve it (chapter 3); and we show you, step by step, how to develop your own program of endurance exercise—probably the most beneficial type of exercise for your overall well-being (chapter 8). A complete set of tables listing common sources of vitamins and minerals, now provided at the end of the book, will help guide you in your meal planning and dietary habits.

There is one thought in particular we would like to leave you with when you have completed this book: Physical fitness is not a miracle and is not a thing to be purchased with money; physical fitness is the result of an attitude of self-responsibility. You are the only person ultimately responsible for your body's care and health. Blame no one else for the shape you are in. Avoid self-pity and self-neglect. Instead, make action and readiness a part of your life and take control. Life is what you make it—and you *can* make it! Remember this as you follow our exercise plan, and you will be successful.

ACKNOWLEDGMENTS

Of the many individuals whose comments helped shape this new edition, we would like to single out for thanks Jean Couch; Jean Lewis, University of Tennessee; Walter Rilliet, Skyline College; and Emilyn Ann Sheffield, University of Southern California, for their detailed critiques of our book.

Be it remembered that until woman comes to her kingdom physically, she will never really come at all. Created to be well and strong and beautiful, she long ago sacrificed her constitution. She has walked when she should have run, sat when she should have walked, reclined when she should have sat. She is a creature born to beauty and freedom.

—EDWARD BELLAMY

CHAPTER 1

The Beginning

The past is but the beginning of a
beginning, and all that is and has
been is but the twilight of the dawn.

—H. G. WELLS

You and your world

The world around us is a fast moving, ever changing kaleidoscope. Society is complex, technology is complex, and both are rapidly becoming ever more intricate. Today we are bombarded with myriad theories about everything, each with the sound of absolute authority, only to discover tomorrow that they have been replaced by a new set of equally convincing "truths." Indeed, *change* has become the most characteristic condition of the modern environment.

What does this have to do with beginning a program of physical fitness? In searching for an appropriate life style, a balance must be struck between new ideas and past wisdom. A good beginning is to explore the interrelationship of mind and body and how each contributes to living life to its fullest. When in balance, mind and body contribute to the development of a complete person. An awareness of the potential and needs of each aspect of personality — intellectual, emotional, spiritual, and physical — is necessary for personal growth and success in life.

You must understand that you can control your achievements by determining your individual life style. The optimum is a choice of life style that leads to the development of the total human being. Life styles are created out of the attitudes with which you face life. If you are looking for a fulfilled, satisfying life, you must develop your ability to adapt to change.

As you go through this program, also think about the cost of society's current fascination with modern conveniences. As we rely more on the ease of living provided by technology, we find ourselves faced with a growing number of health problems stemming from failure to promote the proper functioning of muscles, hearts, and lungs. Problems stem not only from neglect but from flagrant mistreatment. In the United States today, obesity is a health problem of epidemic proportions. The effects of alcohol, prescription drugs, and the common cigarette upon bodies and minds have become a national concern. Heart disease (not "attacks" but the serious harm wrought upon the heart by improper life style) is now the most frequent cause of death. Repeated scientific studies point to the fact that the average daily routine does not include enough activity to tax someone physically or to make positive use of the amounts of food consumed in a day.

As technological change occurs, our bodies remain a constant. We must relearn the structure and chemistry of the human body; learn to evaluate the effects of new external forces upon the nerves, organs, and flesh; and establish a pattern of care for the body which will give them the best physical armament with which to meet the world of today. We must always remain aware of the cost of technology in terms of our physical beings. To be able to sit and watch television is fine, but we must be aware of what will happen if we do not plan activities to counteract the time we spend sitting. If we are to reap the rewards that life has to offer, we must learn to use the advances of technology wisely, and must keep in mind the importance of daily physical exercise and dietary habits that correspond to physical demands.

You in search of self

Today's woman has been deeply affected by recent social change. Woman's potential now seems infinitely greater than it was even a decade ago. It is with excitement that women are discovering themselves as vitally important human beings and recognizing that their goals no longer need be proscribed by traditional definitions of femininity. The door is opening for women to use those talents and ambitions which they possess.

A realistic perception of self in terms of attitudes, needs, aspirations, and capabilities is a necessary accomplishment in learning to live effectively. The woman emerging on the modern scene will emphasize her individual strengths and express her personal values in a much broader sense than ever before. It requires courage and conviction on her part to assume a new identity and accept the accompanying responsibilities. The demands on women in our society are being intensified. The woman of today must be physically ready to live with the pressures these demands will bring.

Regardless of the particular path or paths you have chosen — student, wife, mother, career woman, adventurer — as you analyze your daily routine, you will see that modern technology has limited, to a great degree, your world of physical experience. Lack of physical activity is one of the reasons women have problems maintaining good health and fitness.

Take the case of the student, whether she is a girl in her teens or a woman returning to college after many years. The mental processes of thinking do not burn calories. This person must learn to balance food intake and activity when priority must be given to studies, when many hours must be spent quietly listening, reading, writing. Many students find that the pressure of deadlines and exams causes them to nibble on snacks or to overeat. These are habits that can be controlled by an awareness of body need and habit. A common complaint of dormitory life is the starchiness of the food served in the campus dining commons. The dorm student must learn to select her food carefully. Incidentally, several campus cafeterias and snack bars have recognized this problem and now provide special, low-calorie meals.

The woman running a household assumes the major responsibility of feeding her family. Because men and growing children burn calories at a faster rate than most women, their food needs are greater.[1] With food at her fingertips much of the time, she must develop strong will power to resist the temptation to snack. She must discipline herself to eat what is necessary for her body's physical needs. This is not a superhuman task; it is awareness, discipline, and determination. Most of the homemaker's household jobs consist of small movements that do not burn many calories, even though they may seem exhausting. For instance, cooking, washing dishes, and dusting have been calculated at using only two or three calories per minute.[2] In a well-designed home equipped with refrigerator, washer, dryer, and vacuum cleaner, the task of housework can no longer be considered a physically taxing job. The fatigue many housewives experience comes less from physical exertion than from the frustrations of a daily routine of chores. Introduce into her life the healthful stimulation of all her body resources through a tension-releasing, personalized set of fitness exercises and see her bloom! In addition, time and a place for rest and creative interests must be a part of each woman's life so she can rejuvenate her own mind and body.

The career woman may also tend to neglect her personal needs. Determined to subsist independently, she may leave little time and energy at the end of each working day for preparing a proper meal, let alone for physical activity and exercise. Weekends are precious, saved for shopping excursions and errands she didn't find time for during the week. Yet today's working woman must compensate for the hours of inactivity.

Until recently, just being born female in America meant the disadvantage of an upbringing and environment that limited women's physical activity and, as a result, their confidence about physical pursuits. In the past, boys were taught to be active while girls were taught to be passive and were not taught the joy and freedom which comes from using physical strengths and abilities.

Few experiences reinforcing the concept of physically active lives were provided for girls—and attitudes necessary to motivate women throughout their lives are the result of early childhood experiences.

Now it is easy to understand why many women do not identify with, or even clearly perceive, the physical experience of living. Susan Edminston, in an article explaining the growing awareness among women of a more active type of living, has written: "There is a shift of perspective that takes place, a shift from doing things *to* your body—painting, clothing or starving it—to doing things *with* it, and a corresponding change from passivity to activity."[3] Women can sit back and accept life the way it has been handed to them, or they can assume the task of directing their lives toward the goals they choose. The fitness they desire and are capable of having will not just happen. There are no fairy godmothers in the real world to wave their magic wands and make women instantly slim and beautiful. But there is a very real and powerful force deep within women, if only they take the time to find it and cultivate it. The discipline of will power and the force of self-respect exist in all women simply waiting to be set free.

Paying the price

It takes a great deal of thought, preparation, and work to gain success and satisfaction in reaching your goals. In approaching figure control, you must establish a plan for reaching your goals, and it must be a lifelong plan. Your plan will be only as effective as the strength of your commitment to follow it. A commitment requires an investment of time and energy and a willingness to make personal sacrifices.

When you have arrived at the point of converting thought into action, the task ahead will not be easy—that is a fact you must accept in the beginning if you are to experience success in figure control. You will probably have to change several personal habits and preferences.

Far too often women forego judgment, knowledge, and past experience in attempting to control their figures. Personal opinions and impulses control behavior. Learning to accept change and acknowledging the relationship between cause and effect are possibly the most important steps to a successful experience in figure control.

Your motivation must be strong enough to allow for making changes in your life style. Make every effort to identify the interests, needs, and problems from which your motives are derived so that you can establish the practice of reinforcing them at regular intervals. You must also make certain that this is something you *want* to do.

The woman who is successful in maintaining her figure throughout her lifetime makes a serious commitment to the project. She is creative in adjusting her habits to meet her needs and interests. She sets realistic goals with respect for her limitations. Her goals are not extreme and she does not undertake to solve all problems at once. Each intermediate goal in the long-range picture is a small victory reinforcing her motivation and level of confidence.

It would be wrong to tell you that you will never experience failure or setbacks. You must learn to accept a measure of failure, for you will fail many times before experiencing the sought-for results. When you fall, learn to pick yourself up, brush yourself off, and get back on the road again. Look up, not down. Try to handle your disappointments and failures with tolerance. Recognize, define, and solve problems, and attempt to follow through with new ideas and new approaches. Control your impulses with knowledge and reasoning. Learn to delay immediate satisfactions as you look toward the success you will experience in accomplishing the goals you have established.

Life is full of choices and decisions. Women can choose to "let nature take its course" or can choose to control their lives by accepting the responsibility for their decisions. The freedom to make wise choices comes from discipline. Self-discipline is one key to success in any endeavor; this is absolutely true in the realm of figure control. To maintain a good figure, a healthy mind, and a strong body you must be prepared to pay the price—in time, hard work, and determination.

Finally, enough cannot be said about the importance of keeping a positive outlook. Strive for enthusiasm in every task you undertake. Far too many women allow negative ideas to frustrate their most constructive goals. The burden of discovering your happiness rests with you. Keep your thought processes constantly alert, appreciate your own efforts and your strengths, accept the reality of change, and know when and how you must adjust to it. Remember, it's your future you're building!

Notes

1 Sue Rodwell Williams, *Nutrition and Diet Therapy* (St. Louis: C.V. Mosby, 1969), p. 68.

2 L. Jean Bogert, George M. Briggs, and Doris H. Calloway, *Nutrition and Physical Fitness* (Philadelphia: W.B. Saunders, 1973) p. 40.

3 Susan Edminston, "The Gymsuit Blues; Changing the Odds Against Women," *Redbook Magazine,* January 1974, p. 125.

CHAPTER 2

Paths of Reality

Two roads diverged in a wood, and I—
I took the one less traveled by,
And that has made all the difference.

—ROBERT FROST

The desire for an attractive figure is a very real thing to each woman. The media barrage of products, services, and books related to weight control and figure contouring is convincing evidence of this fact. As consumers, women are willing to buy all kinds of gimmicks and gadgets guaranteed to help them in their quest. All of us look for an easy way to solve problems, choosing to believe there is a quick and simple solution.

If you have a figure problem, chances are you have been seduced by at least one of the effortless methods offered to today's affluent consumer who spends or sends money with the hopeful attitude, "I'll try anything once!" Actually, what you are buying is the idea that there is a magic formula for achieving the ideal figure. More effort goes in to making a believer out of you than in helping you achieve the figure you desire. Some of the more common uses of guile and gimmickry are described in the following paragraphs.

The promise of losing inches in only one visit to a figure salon or health spa is a very effective way to attract paying customers. How satisfying it is to see astounding results in measurements after your very first visit! But think about it: A tape measure can be very easily manipulated. It can be placed higher or lower on your body or held loosely or tightly, and the person measuring you can easily place one or two fingers under the tape while pulling it together behind your back. And when a measurement is taken at the conclusion of your visit, you can be reminded to stand very tall and hold yourself erect so you can be measured at your best. Try this trick yourself, and you will see that the inches melt away before your eyes! This is because posture improvement alone will show improvement in measurements taken at the bustline, waist, and hips.

But if we can be impressed with the idea that taking off those extra inches isn't going to be as hard as we imagined, we may consider taking out a membership with the salon. If so, here's another caution: Look before you sign that contract. Is it for one year, two years, or three? There is no way to get out of paying for an unused portion of time. And notice that these types of salons do not guarantee *weight loss* — for a very good reason. It is impossible to manipulate the scale because the customer can read it herself.

Studios that provide wrapping treatments guarantee loss of inches. Their method is a simple one indeed, based on the displacement of fluid in the body and the loss of fluid from the body. Immediately after the unwrapping, measurements show a loss of inches. You will "lose inches," but this is not permanent loss of fatty tissue; it is merely fluid loss, and as soon as you resume normal activity and consume liquids, you will return to your original measurements. The water-loss myth is one of the most widespread fallacies about weight control. It is *never* more than temporary weight loss, however, regardless of the device used to produce it. Most commonly found among these devices are diuretic pills, sweat and sauna suits, wrapping, and steam baths.

Some salons provide equipment that "does the work for you." Also, you can purchase equipment for home use which advertisements claim can tone your muscles while you relax. Two of these machines should be labeled hazardous: the vibrator-belt and the roller machine, which can damage the skin and tissues by bruising and causing stretch-marks. These machines also have very little real effect and are a waste of time and money.

Among the most ridiculous gimmicks sold to women are the bust-developers, "guaranteed" to increase breast size. The breast is made up of glandular and fatty tissue and the two things affecting its size are heredity and weight. There are no muscles which can be exercised and developed within the breast; thus there is no way to change its size other then through surgery. The muscles lying under the breast, forming the chest wall, can be exercised. The result will strengthen support and minimize bra bulges.

Consumer fascination with exercise gimmicks and body shapers is surpassed only by the incredible number of methods for weight control. There are doctors, drugs, foods, clubs, menus, recipes, and magazines entirely devoted to diet and weight control. Countless fad diets sweep through the country regularly, emphasizing the fact that more than half the American population is said to be concerned with excess weight. This is a concern that large manufacturers and unscrupulous professionals alike have capitalized on.

People seldom take the time to check further than the brand name if the word "diet" is attached to the label. We want to believe that certain foods contain no calories because they are labeled as such. Good examples are the "diet breads" on the market. White enriched diet bread contains an average of seven calories per ounce as compared to regular white enriched bread at eight calories per ounce — only a one-calorie difference. A slice of diet bread is lower in calories simply because of thin slicing. A similar technique is used with recipes and menus. The "diet-label" is attached when the calorie content is only slightly adjusted to provide fewer calories. To make matters worse, we tend to justify larger or additional servings of food just because we are told they are lower in calories. Learning to check labels for contents is a big step in consumer education.

The group motivation of "diet clubs" provides the necessary incentive for some people to lose weight. However, it can be expensive, time-consuming, and next to impossible for the working woman. A comment commonly heard from people using this method is, "I spend most of the day either shopping or cooking." If the diet organization subscribes to the concept that exercise is detrimental to your diet, you may assume that it intends to keep you around longer, meanwhile charging you periodic membership dues. Diet organizations, however, can be beneficial to the person wanting to learn good nutritional concepts and establish better eating habits. Use good judgment when selecting a diet organization or club.

In addition, women are turning in increasing numbers to "diet clinics" where doctors under the cloak of professional respectability are prescribing all kinds of pills and injections. Some pills actually do curb the appetite for a period of time, but many are habit-forming and dangerous in the long run. Paying for pills or injections is certainly not a wise lifetime plan for controlling weight.

You must keep in mind that weight control and figure control are not short-term tasks. Lifetime goals must be established. What happens when the diet ends or you stop taking the pills? The greatest feeling of security and satisfaction comes from knowing that you have the power, the determination and self-discipline, to accomplish by yourself the goals you set.

CHAPTER 3

Nutrition
and Weight Control

Individuals may have little control
over . . . the environment, but they
have a great deal of control over their
own behavior. No one has more power
than you have to determine whether
you drink too much . . . or overeat.

—PAUL INSEL and WALTON ROTH
Health in a Changing Society (1976)

Proper nutrition is one of the most important aspects of healthful living.
Although almost everyone is interested in nutrition today, few are really
knowledgeable about the relationship of nutrition, exercise, weight control,
and physiological conditioning. This leaves women vulnerable to the unscrupulous and dishonest entrepreneurs who stand to make financial gain through
misinformation, distortion, and incorrect application of nutritional concepts.
A large segment of our population has, as its primary interest, the selling of
special foods and dietary supplements. This can lead to the exploitation of
women's limited knowledge in nutrition by arguments that seem reasonable,
but which have little regard for honesty or truth.[1]

This chapter explores the role of nutrition as it relates to basic health,
physical activity, and weight control. We must begin with the fact that nutrition is a science based on the food requirements of the body. Even though the
human body will operate and survive on any number of foods, scientific
knowledge shows that there are specific combinations of foods that allow our
bodies to operate most efficiently.

The nutrients

Food contains nutrients, the chemical compounds that provide the energy
necessary for the human body to function. Nutrients are utilized to maintain

and build body tissues and regulate body processes and supply heat, thereby sustaining life.[2] Although there are over fifty nutrients, they can be divided into six major classifications according to their chemical structure. Each nutrient has its specific function; however, it is the total combination of nutrients that is essential to the efficient functioning of the human body.

Water   Water is second only to oxygen as a vital support for life. The body can go for weeks without food but only a few days without water. In addition to the water in tissues and cells, the body's blood supply contains about four quarts of water. Water is excreted continuously by sweating and through urine, and it must be constantly replaced. Replacement comes through water and other fluids such as milk, soups, and drinks, and even through the moisture in solid foods such as fruits. Some fruits and vegetables contain as much as 85 percent water. Moisture is even found in solid foods like meat and breads.

Water is used as a solvent in the digestive processes, where it aids the chewing and softening of food.[3] It is used during the digestion process, for the elimination of the by-products of cell metabolism (waste products), and for control of body temperature.[4] In addition, water provides fluid for joint lubrication, cells, intestines, the brain, and the spinal cord. The fluid in the inner ear promotes hearing as well as balance. Water is also needed to provide the fluids in the eyes and lungs. The human body, in fact, contains almost two-thirds water. Water is so essential for life that a water loss of 10 percent of total body weight is quite serious, while a loss of 20 percent may result in death.

A loss of body fluid is considerable, even when engaging in light physical activity. Therefore, you must be concerned about fluid intake during any kind of activity. Even low humidity will result in an increased need for water. Water cannot be stored within the body; therefore, you must strive never to get into situations where it is not readily available. The importance of water to health and well-being cannot be overstressed.

Protein   Protein provides the amino acids that are essential to the building and growth of new tissues, tissue maintenance and repair, the production of enzymes and certain hormones, the production of milk, and as an alternate source of energy. Amino acids are organic compounds which make up protein—twenty in number. Of the twenty, eight are known as *essential*. They must be supplied by food since they cannot be synthesized in the body at a sufficient rate to prevent an impairment in normal cellular function.[5] A protein that supplies all eight of the essential amino acids is called a *complete* protein. The body needs these eight amino acids in a certain proportion. Other proteins are labeled *incomplete* proteins.

The amino acids essential to the human body are valine, lysine, threonine, leucine, isoleucine, tryptophan, phenylalanine, and methionine. One other amino acid, histidine, is required by infants, and recent research suggests that it may also be essential for adults.[6] The other amino acids are nonessential, which does not imply that they are not needed but that they can be synthesized within the tissues from other foods including other amino acids.

Protein is found in all living animal and plant life. Complete proteins are eggs, milk, meat, fish, and poultry. Incomplete proteins will be discussed more thoroughly in the section on vegetarianism. As a rule, Americans consume too much protein. If the dietary amount of fat and carbohydrate is sufficient, then just a small amount of high-quality protein is needed for an adult—approximately 8 to 9 percent of the total daily calories.[7] An increased level of protein is recommended for infants, children, and pregnant or lactating women. The protein consumed should be of the highest quality, such as found in egg or milk.[8] As the quality of protein decreases, the quantity must increase. It is recommended that an adult receive one-third or more of the protein from complete protein foods, and a child from one-half to two-thirds of the protein from animal sources.[9]

Carbohydrate Carbohydrate is not only the most economical source of energy, but also the major source. It is also the most abundant nutrient found in food. Carbohydrates can be divided into three types—monosaccharides, disaccharides, and polysaccharides.

Monosaccharides are the simple sugars—glucose, fructose, and galactose. With the exception of galactose, they occur free in foods such as fruits and vegetables. Galactose is a result of the digestion of lactose.

Disaccharides, the double sugars, are sucrose, lactose, and maltose. Sucrose, or table sugar, comes primarily from sugar cane and beets, maple sugar and syrup, molasses, and, in small amounts, from fruits and vegetables. Maltose, also called malt sugar, is a product of the digestion of starches. Lactose, sometimes referred to as milk sugar, comes from both animal and human milk and is less easy to digest. Lactose is also not as sweet as other sugars.

Polysaccharides are the very complex sugars—starch, dextrins, glycogen, and cellulose. Starch comes from seeds, grains, root and tuber vegetables, and legumes and must be cooked in order to be fully digestible. The dextrins occur as a result of the digestion of starch. Glycogen is formed when extra amounts of glucose are present in the blood, with the formation occurring primarily in the liver and muscles.[10] Glycogen is the human body's method of storing carbohydrate. It can be converted into glucose for use when the body needs it. Cellulose is the framework for the structural part of plants. The best sources are whole grains, dried fruits, nuts, vegetables, and fresh fruits. It serves in our diet as a source of bulk.

There is no definite requirement for carbohydrates in a good diet; however, carbohydrate does "spare" protein as sources of energy. Carbohydrates are also needed to completely oxidize the fat in a diet. Since glucose is essentially the only form of energy available to the brain, carbohydrates are needed for the proper functioning of the central nervous system.[11] Keep in mind that the pure carbohydrates such as sugar, syrups, jelly, and cornstarch, contribute little to the nutritive value in a diet. They are "empty calories," and their intake should be restricted.

Fats   Fats, also called lipids, are found in both animals and plants. They are the most concentrated sources of energy. Fats serve as carriers of the fat-soluble vitamins and are the only sources of linoleic acid. They are also important in making food more palatable and for their satiety value.

Fat is actually a combination of glycerol and varying amounts of saturated, monounsaturated, and polyunsaturated fatty acids and is classified according to the dominant fatty acid.[12] Saturated fats tend to be hard and come primarily from animals, while the unsaturated fats come from vegetables in liquid or semiliquid form.

The terms *cholesterol* and *triglyceride* are common in today's vocabulary, especially in reference to heart disease. All animal fats contain cholesterol in varying degrees. Cholesterol is a fat-related substance which is a normal component of most body tissues, especially those of the brain, nervous system, liver, and blood.[13] Since the body can manufacture cholesterol within the liver, it does not need to be added to the diet. Triglyceride is simply a name that describes a type of fat molecule. Triglycerides compose 95 percent of the body's fat intake, while less than 5 percent is cholesterol. Cholesterol may be less important as a factor in heart disease than people have recently been led to believe.[14] Some researchers believe that physical activity is more important than either the amount or kind of fat in the diet.[15] Other factors such as obesity, stress, high blood pressure, and heavy cigarette smoking are also important areas of risk in heart disease. Research has not yet isolated the one factor most important to preventing heart disease, so keep in mind that a combination of factors definitely increases the risk of heart disease.

Vitamins   Vitamins help regulate the chemical processes of the body. They are required in very small amounts but must be replaced frequently since the body does not manufacture them. Vitamins are divided into two major groups. The fat-soluble vitamins (A, D, E, and K) are, as a general rule, associated with foods containing fat and are stored with the fat in the body. They are not usually destroyed by cooking but can become rancid. The excessive use of fat-soluble vitamins can result in a toxic condition, since these vitamins are largely stored within the body. Water-soluble vitamins (B-complex and C) are absorbed directly into the bloodstream, where they are either utilized by the body or eliminated by the kidneys. Toxicity, therefore, is not likely to occur from the use of water-soluble vitamins. The value of these vitamins can be affected by cooking methods, especially by discarding the water or liquid in which they were cooked or soaked.[16]

Vitamin deficiencies are not likely to occur if following a well-balanced diet. Vitamins are among the most over-consumed products on the market, and many people are falling for the "natural is better" cry of the vendor. The *megavitamin* theories have not been proven by scientific research, nor has the theory that large amounts of vitamins enhance physical performance in sports. The daily requirements for vitamins are relatively independent of a person's physical activity level.[17]

Consumers are led to believe that vitamins are nutrients and they can't consume too much of a good thing, but evidence is beginning to show otherwise. Large doses of vitamin C have been known to destroy vitamin B-12 in foods and cause kidney stones in susceptible people, while large doses of vitamin E have caused headaches, nausea, giddiness, fatigue, and blurred vision.[18] Excessive vitamin E may also cause a deficiency in vitamin K, needed for normal clotting of the blood.[19] In addition to vitamin E, other fat-soluble vitamins have caused problems when taken excessively. Retarded growth has resulted in some children after consuming excessive amounts of vitamin D. The same vitamin in large dosages has caused some adults to experience kidney damage. Vitamin A has been known to cause indigestion, nausea, and diarrhea as well as headaches. In mega-doses, many vitamins cannot perform their natural function but instead act like drugs.[20]

There is no magic in vitamins, and when taken to excess they can be dangerous. Children should be cautioned against taking handfuls of vitamin "charms and animals," as well as any other type of medicine. Adults should not consume vitamins unless prescribed by a physician. Refer to Appendix C for a complete chart on the characteristics and food sources of vitamins and symptoms of vitamin deficiencies.

Minerals Minerals are inorganic substances of a simple structure, unlike vitamins, which are organic compounds containing the element carbon. Minerals always retain their structure and are indestructible; cooking does not have an effect on them. Certain minerals are water soluble and are readily absorbed into the bloodstream where they are either utilized by the body or eliminated. Others are fat soluble and toxic conditions can result if they are taken in excess. The mineral or metallic elements make up approximately 5 percent of body weight, and each is vital for proper cell functioning.[21]

Minerals are divided into two major classifications. The *major* minerals, or *macronutrient* elements, are needed in greater proportion than the *trace* minerals, or *micronutrient* elements.[22] In both cases, however, the amounts are minute in comparison to the requirements for other nutrients. A well-balanced diet will supply the minerals needed for proper body functioning. Additional information on minerals, including sources, requirements, and symptoms of deficiencies, is given in Appendix C.

The essentials of a well-balanced diet

A well-balanced diet meets the body's need for the nutrients previously discussed. These needs can be met in a variety of ways, taking into consideration cultural preferences, taste, economic conditions, environment, and the availability of foods. The diet, however, must meet certain guidelines relating to the general classes of foods discussed on the following pages and summarized in Figure 3-1. With very few exceptions, most dietary requirements will be met by selecting foods from these groups.

Milk and milk products   Foods from the milk group supply most of the calcium requirement in a diet. In addition, they provide riboflavin, other vitamins and minerals, high-quality protein, carbohydrate, and fat.[23] The foods include all types of fluid milk, cheese (including cottage cheese), ice cream and ice milk, and yogurt. Two servings of the milk group are considered sufficient for adults. Growing children, including teenagers and pregnant and lactating women should increase this requirement by one or two servings. One serving is equivalent to one cup of milk, one-and-one-third ounces of cheese, one-and-one-third cups of cottage cheese, one-and-two-thirds cups of ice cream or ice milk, or one cup of yogurt.

Meat products   The meat group provides high-quality protein, fat, and many vitamins and minerals. Foods in this group that contain all of the amino acids needed for proper functioning of the body include beef, lamb, pork, poultry, fish, eggs, and other wild or domestic animal meat products. Two servings of meat daily are considered sufficient for most individuals of all ages. A serving is equal to three ounces of meat or two eggs. Salt pork, fatback, and bacon are considered fat and not meat.[24] Alternatives to meat eating are discussed in the section on vegetarianism.

Vegetables and fruits   Besides carbohydrates, the vegetable and fruit group supplies fiber to the diet, oils, and many vitamins and minerals. The minimum daily requirements are, in five areas: dark green and yellow vegetables, one-half cup; potatoes, one medium; tomatoes and other vegetables, one-third cup; citrus fruits, one-half cup; other fruits, one-half cup.

Cereals and breads   The cereals and breads group is a high-carbohydrate group which also meets the requirements for many vitamins and minerals. The daily requirement is three to four servings. A serving is one slice of bread or three-fourths cup of cereal.

1. **Milk or milk products** (2 or more servings). One cup of milk or yogurt, or one and a third cups of cottage cheese, or two or three scoops of ice cream, or a serving of hard cheese (such as cheddar) equal to about a one-inch cube.

2. **High-protein foods** (2 or more servings). A serving is a three-ounce portion of any meat, fish, or poultry, or two eggs. These foods can be alternated with a cup of dry peas of dry beans or lentils, with four tablespoons of peanut butter, or with the 60-odd nuts used to make the peanut butter. Cheese may also be used here if it is not used in the milk group.

3. **Green or yellow vegetables** (2 servings). A half cup is a typical serving. Dark green or deep yellow vegetables are the best sources of the several nutrients supplied by these foods.

4. **Citrus fruits, tomatoes, and other good sources of vitamin C** (1 serving). A serving is six ounces of citrus juice, with more of tomato juice preferred, an orange or a half a grapefruit, two generous cups of frozen lemonade, or a medium tomato. Two thirds of a cup of strawberries can be a replacement, a sixth of a medium watermelon, or half a papaya. Or, if you have extra servings from some foods in the vegetable group, they can be applied here, in one-cup amounts: raw cabbage, collards, kale, kohlrabi, mustard greens, spinach, and turnip greens.

5. **Potatoes and other vegetables and fruits** (1 serving). A serving is a medium potato, an ear of corn, an apple, or a banana; it is usually about a half a cup of such items as cooked, canned, or raw carrots, peaches, pineapple, apricots, beets, lima beans, cauliflower, or a small salad portion of lettuce.

6. **Bread, flour, and cereals** (3-4 servings). One serving is a slice of bread, an ounce of ready-to-eat breakfast cereal, one-half to three-fourths of a cup of cooked breakfast cereal, cornmeal, grits, macaroni, noodles, rice, spaghetti, a two-inch biscuit, three-inch cookie, slice of cake, or muffin. (All baked goods should be made with enriched or whole-grain flour; otherwise they may not do their job in this group.) A doughnut, a four-inch pancake, or half a waffle will also serve.

7. **Butter or margarine** (2-3 servings). A serving is a tablespoon.

8. **Fluids** (3-5 servings). A serving is one cup and includes primarily water-based drinks, such as water, milk, fruit juice, beer, coffee, tea, powdered mixes, carbonated soft drinks.

9. **Sugar foods** (none needed). One serving is interpreted as three teaspoons of added sugar (as to coffee, fruit), a half-ounce of hard candy, marshmallow, or carmel, and slightly more chocolate. One tablespoon of honey, molasses, two one-inch mints, a tablespoon of syrup (chocolate, maple, corn, etc.), jam or jelly.

Figure 3-1 The Essentials of a Well-balanced Diet

What about sugar?

Americans consume a great deal of sugar—over one hundred pounds a year by the average American. It is difficult not to consume sugar! Read the labels in your grocery market and you will find that most processed foods contain additional sugar. You have to really be on your toes to stay away from it.

There is no evidence to show that sugar is in any way poisonous to the normal, healthy human being.[25] However, it can have some harmful side effects. It can be a contributing factor to tooth decay, obesity, diabetes, and a loss of appetite for the proper nutrients. The greatest single problem associated with a high sugar intake is that sugar contributes only empty calories.[26] Sugar has very little nutritive value. When you substitute complex carbohydrates for sugars, the mineral and vitamin content of your diet is improved.[27]

In attempting to avoid refined sugar, many consumers turn to natural, raw, or brown sugar, accepting the line of the advertiser that these have more nutrients.[28] These sugars are no better—they are also empty calories. You should, instead, substitute fruits because of their nutritive value and their ability to satisfy a "sweet tooth." Honey and molasses have no special nutritive value. Honey contains glucose and fructose, the same simple sugars present in table sugar.[29] The fact that molasses is very dark gives it no real extra nutritive value.

Sugar has been linked to coronary heart disease, although the evidence is not strong enough to establish it as a contributing factor.[30] In one study, animals on a sugar-only diet suffered side effects of impaired growth and showed high levels of cholesterol and triglycerides in the bloodstream.[31] However, there is no corresponding research on human beings.

Sugar can be a factor in tooth decay, but so can other carbohydrates and other foods. Actually, sticky foods contribute more to tooth decay than any other kind of food. Sugar does contribute to obesity, as do other foods. Sugar may play a more important role because sweet foods taste so good. They cause us to feel full and are somewhat addictive in taste, resulting in an increased desire for sweet foods.

Vegetarianism

The number of vegetarians in America today is on the increase, with explanations of the phenomenon ranging from the influence of Eastern religions to humanitarian feelings.[33] However, the reason cited by most individuals for not eating meat is health.[34]

Many people feel that a meatless diet is more healthful. Although evidence does not fully support this theory, studies of Seventh Day Adventists (who do not eat meat) provide some support. Males were shown to have lower serum cholesterol values and their incidence of heart disease was only 60 percent as high as that of a control group.[35] A distinct advantage for the weight conscious is that a true vegetarian diet is usually lower in calories. Because of the amount of fiber in their diets, vegetarians have also been found to be less likely to suffer from constipation.[36] The evidence, however, is not conclusive. We do not know whether the evidence is the result of vegetarian diets or the fact that most of the people in the studies also said they do not smoke or drink alcoholic beverages. The human being is so complex and eating habits so diverse that to pin complicated and poorly understood diseases on eating patterns is virtually impossible.[37]

Types of vegetarians   There are different types of vegetarians. The individual diet that is completely devoid of animal products is rare. All vegetarians are not "health nuts," subsisting solely on what they believe to be organic foods. Some avoid only red meats, others include dairy products, and some are only "occasional" vegetarians. This last group eats meat on certain occasions, such as on holidays. For this reason, vegetarians are usually divided into four groups—the true vegan, the lacto vegetarian, the lacto-ovo vegetarian, and the occasional vegetarian. The latter group will not be discussed in detail since these individuals also fit into the other groups.

   The true vegan eats only plant foods and no animal products. Even within this classification there are variations. There are people who subsist only on grain products; individuals who eat only vegetable, fruit, and grain products; and individuals who follow a fruitarian diet consisting of raw and dried fruits, nuts, honey, and oil.[38] A strict vegetarian diet can be adequate if the foods are carefully selected; however, some of the variations are seriously lacking in certain amino acids, vitamins, and minerals.

   The lacto-vegetarian supplements the vegetarian diet with milk products. This includes milk in all of its forms—cheese, yogurt, cottage cheese, and so forth. The well-selected lacto-vegetarian diet is nutritionally sound.

   The lacto-ovo vegetarian, in addition to eating all plant foods, will also eat all milk and dairy products, including eggs. Some individuals from this group also eat fish and poultry. Since these people can consume foods from every food group, it is not difficult to meet nutritional standards. The diet of lacto-ovo vegetarians is really not that different from that of many nonvegetarians. There are individuals who don't even identify themselves as vegetarians who fit into this catagory.

Problems associated with vegetarian diets   A nutritionally adequate diet is usually a problem for only the true vegan. Since lacto and lacto-ovo vegetarians supplement their vegetable diet with milk products, problems should not occur as a result of their food intake.

   Serious problems can occur as a result of the diet of a strict vegetarian. Caloric intake can be inadequate, resulting in severe weight loss. Protein intake can be insufficient, resulting in a deficiency of certain amino acids. The human body cannot efficiently utilize the iron from plant food so, if meats are eliminated, the body will usually suffer an iron deficiency unless the diet is carefully planned. In addition, the absence of milk from the diet can cause a calcium deficiency. A deficiency in vitamin B-12 is characteristic of all vegan diets, since the vitamin is found only in animal food.[39] Unless exposure to sunshine is included in the vegan's routine, a vitamin D deficiency can result as well.

Dietary planning to prevent deficiencies   The *caloric* intake of the strict vegan must be carefully observed, especially in the beginning. New vegetarians are most likely to suffer the consequences of the ill-planned vegetarian diet. After good dietary habits have been established, close observation is not as necessary. At the beginning, a diary of daily food intake should be kept, and calculation of the number of calories consumed and the types of foods eaten should be done on a daily basis. If nutrients are missing or the daily food intake is short on calories, an adjustment can be made the next day.

The *vitamin and mineral* charts in Appendix C can be used to insure that proper amounts and correct foods are included in the daily diet plan. Keep in mind that legumes (especially soybeans), whole grains, leafy green vegetables, and dried fruit are good plant sources of iron, while milk and eggs are poor sources.[40] Cooking in cast-iron pots is an excellent way to obtain iron. Calcium and riboflavin amounts will be adequate if the diet includes broccoli, collard greens, or kale. Other greens supply riboflavin, but the oxalic acid in them makes the calcium unabsorbable.[41] The zinc that might be missing from the diet can be supplied by legumes and grains. Fortified cereals will alleviate a vitamin B-12 deficiency, and the missing vitamin D can be corrected with adequate exposure to sunshine.

Protein intake is the biggest obstacle to overcome in planning the strict vegetarian diet. If the daily food intake is not carefully considered, certain amino acids will be missing. The adult requirement is approximately one gram for each two pounds of body weight, while a child needs almost two grams per pound of body weight. Certain vegetables and grains can be combined to form a complete protein containing all of the essential amino acids. For example, when rice is eaten with beans, the missing amino acid of the beans (methionine) is supplied by the rice, and the missing amino acid of the rice (lysine) is supplied by the beans.[42] Soybeans alone are a complete protein, but legumes and grains form a complete protein as do cornbread and beans, and blackeyed or crowder peas and rice. Peanut butter when combined with bread forms a complete protein. It is imperative, however, that the combinations be consumed during the same meal.[43] If the amino acids cannot combine, then a complete protein does not result.

In addition to the combinations, commercial vegetable protein foods are available today. *Consumer Reports* magazine lists, among others, vegetarian fillets, vegeburgers, millet stew, and meatless sloppy joe. The problem with most of these commercial products is their expense. With a little ingenuity, you can prepare your own meatless "meat" by using combinations of vegetables and grains. The vegan, then, must be well informed and choose foods carefully. If foods are selected according to their nutrient value, the strict vegetarian's diet can be healthful.

Weight control

Excess body weight is a major health hazard. Unfortunately it is a condition shared by many Americans. Overweight individuals are more likely to have heart disease, diabetes, and hypertension than slimmer people. In addition, obese people usually suffer more complications from surgery and pregnancy.

There are many definitions of the condition of being overweight, or *obesity*. Most experts agree, though, that it is carrying weight in excess of one's normal range. Of course, the degree of obesity depends upon the amount of extra weight carried. Here the term obese refers to any degree of overweight in excess of 10 percent of the norm.

How is obesity determined?   The most accurate methods for determining the amount of fat in relationship to other body tissue include the needle biopsy, x ray, and underwater weighing, and all require experienced technicians and well-equipped laboratories. Although these methods are impractical for daily body weight determination, they are valuable to research and in severe cases. Measurement using skinfold calipers is a method that can be utilized by knowledgable individuals. However, this method is impractical for most because of the expense of the calipers.

The two most practical methods for the average person are the "image test" and weighing on a regular set of scales. The image test is performed by standing nude in front of a mirror, something rarely done by those who are overweight. The mirror rarely lies! Another practical home method for determining weight is the bathroom scale. Most are reasonably accurate if they are not moved around too much. Make certain the scale is on a solid surface, not resting on carpet, and weigh on the same scale each time you weigh. Don't compare weights on two different scales because all scales are not accurately set. Check your scale against those in your doctor's office, then make necessary adjustments. Weigh in the morning without clothes, right after urinating. Compare your weight against the Average Weight Chart in Appendix A.

What causes obesity?   There are a number of causes of obesity. Although food represents needed energy for the body, there is a limit to how much the body can use. Any excess is stored within the body as fat. Maintaining body weight depends on a precise balance between energy intake and energy expenditure. The factors that disrupt this balance are heredity, environment, emotional disturbances, self-indulgence, sedentary living, misinformation, and ignorance of correct eating habits. Only a small percentage of obesity cases are caused by metabolic disfunctions.

Important in considering the causes of obesity is early childhood training and establishment of eating habits. Research has determined a relationship between the number and size of an individual's fat cells and obesity. During the first year of life, an infant's fat cells triple in number, and most of the fat cells are formed during the final three months of pregnancy prior to birth.[44] The fat cells continue to grow in number during childhood, adolescence, and possibly even into the early twenties. However, growth patterns indicate that the majority of cells are established prior to the thirteenth year. Thus, the critical periods are the final three months of pregnancy, and from the first year of life to the thirteenth year.[45] Studies show that regular exercise begun early in life may reduce the final number of fat cells, keeping the total content of fat reduced in later life.[46] With weight gain, fat cells increase in size, and with weight loss they decrease. The importance of fat cells is the number of cells established in the early growth years.

Whether the cause is organic, psychogenic, or cultural, the factor most directly responsible for obesity is overeating. Overeating can result from any of a variety of factors. The result is like a snowball rolling downhill. Overeating causes weight gain; as weight becomes excessive, the body becomes less efficient and burns fewer calories. Because the body is burning fewer calories, the individual becomes lethargic and doesn't feel like exercising. The exercise not only feels like it requires more effort, but its results are much less apparent to the obese woman, because her figure lies hidden beneath fat. To be sure, the exercise is working, but if its results are not evident, she may give up and, out of discouragement or impatience, resign herself to "fate." Or she may join the thousands of other Americans who support the million-dollar market in health fads and reducing aids.

Fads and reducing aids   Who wouldn't be tempted to seek the effortless, dramatic effects promised by a revolutionary diet plan? New reducing pills and diets seem to be at the height of popularity today. Television advertising is inundated with their commercials; we are all prey to their suggestion. The advertising promises spectacular results with little effort on the user's part.

The problem with reducing pills and diets is generally twofold: They seldom help to establish eating habits necessary for lifelong weight control, and they are nutritionally inadequate. When essential foods and nutrients are supplied irregularly or are left out entirely for a period of time, the body's metabolism may be changed or upset resulting in poor utilization of certain foods. This could cause the individual to gain even more weight once off the diet.

Day:_____

Date:_____

Food	Amount	Calories	Exercise	Amount/Time	Calories

Calorie intake (total food) _____

Calorie expenditure (total exercise) _____

Balance (calorie intake − calorie expenditure = no. of calories) _____

Figure 3-2   Energy Evaluation Diary

For the individual susceptible to a particular nutritional imbalance, the wrong kind of diet may have drastic results. The effect of a high-protein diet on a person with a kidney infection or malfunction could be kidney failure or even death. In addition to the irrational and unsound basis of most fad diets and pills, they are not recommended because of their constant threat to health.

Many pounds have been lost, regained, lost, and regained again on fad reducing diets, pills, and other aids. However, the weight usually does not stay off, resulting in a "yo-yo syndrome." This can be more harmful than remaining overweight. Whether the diet is high or low in carbohydrate or high or low in protein, involves counting calories or counting carbohydrate grams (numerous variations exist), the result is the same. You must consume less fuel than you use in order to lose weight, do the opposite to gain weight, and balance the two in order to maintain body weight. Unfortunately, there is no magical formula, just common sense and nutritional knowledge put to good use.

Calories and metabolism *Calories* and *metabolism* are two terms often used in conjunction with gaining and losing weight. Both have a direct relationship to energy and to food, and it is important to know what they are.

Calories are simply measures of energy (fuel). When the body moves, energy is used. The source of that energy is food. You should use calories to measure food intake and expenditure. One pound of body fat equals 3500 calories.

Metabolism is another term often used in connection with weight control. It is used far too often as an excuse for weight problems. The few cases of obesity that are caused by metabolic disorders should be treated by a physician. Metabolism involves a complex process; it is not a simple excuse. It involves the conversion of fuel to energy and the body's utilization of that energy. The *basic metabolic rate* (BMR) refers to the amount of energy consumed while the body is in a resting state. Remember that changing fuel into energy is nothing more than using calories. Keeping this information in mind, consider some of the facts about weight control and metabolism.

Your metabolic rate drops by about 10 percent when you are sleeping. This tells you to consume the bulk of your calories during active hours and to make the evening meal a light one. A good rule of thumb is to refrain from eating during the four hours before bedtime. The metabolic rate of children and men is higher than that of women, again by approximately 10 percent. You cannot consume the same number of calories as a male and get by with it for very long. Metabolic rate also declines with age, although gradually, indicating that you should eat less and move more as you grow older. Illness and surgery can cause the BMR to increase and the body temperature to rise. Exercise for approximately twenty minutes or more at a fast pace will also result in an increase in the metabolic rate. A decrease in energy intake will affect the energy expenditure, so that during fasting the body's metabolic rate slows.

Since there is no average individual, it is not possible to give an average BMR for women and men. People differ in their activities, work, sleeping habits, health conditions and levels of stress, so it is difficult to make realistic comparisons.

Determining your metabolic range can be accomplished by keeping a diary of daily food intake and your activity expenditure level. This may be tedious, but it must be done for at least one week in order to determine your personal average. Try to be as accurate as possible in measuring your food and in determining your activity. Be sure to include the entire twenty-four hours of the day and night. Purchase a small notebook and use a diary like the one shown in Figure 3-2 to chart each day.

This type of record keeping will show you where to begin. You will want to use the Energy Expenditure Chart (Appendix B) as a guide for determining your activity values. You will need to purchase a good calorie guide in order to count food intake. These may be purchased at many locations, including bookstores, drugstores, and grocery markets.

While keeping in mind that 3500 calories equal one pound of body fat, you must adjust your energy balance accordingly. This may be accomplished by a change in food intake, activity level, or both. Usually, it is best accomplished by adjusting both. A two-pound weight loss per week is considered maximum. A more drastic change might result in an unhealthy condition. In order for this to happen, you must eliminate 1000 calories per day—two waffles with butter and syrup equal 450 calories, and one piece of strawberry pie can be worth approximately 950 calories depending on the amount of whipped cream.

Continue the record keeping as long as you have not met your weight goal. If your tally shows a lower calorie intake than calorie expenditure, you are on your way to weight loss. There will come a time when you will not have to make entries in your diary every day; however, when problems reappear, you should begin using it again.

Final advice for the weight conscious   The science of nutrition, the fundamental knowledge that your body requires certain foods to be nourished and to operate, must be the basis for your eating habits. The phrase *well-balanced diet* refers to a pattern of eating habits which, once established, will see you through a lifetime. It will take time, planning, patience, and effort every day of your life to maintain eating habits that will control your weight.

You must begin with awareness. You must accept the fact that you are overweight and must make some changes in your behavior in order to accomplish your goals. You will have to give in a little and give up a little, sometimes a lot. Becoming aware of the need to change is the first step toward success.

You must begin to develop a food and activity plan, using the material in your records. Develop a sensible plan—one that you can live with and accept. A specific diet or menu cannot be recommended because women are far too different culturally, economically, and emotionally. Your diet and menus must be your own, or you won't be able to follow them.

Now some final suggestions. Eliminate all eating between meals and reduce the tasting of foods that you are preparing. Remember that tasting foods adds calories also. If you consume more calories in one day than you should, adjust your food intake accordingly during the next day; this will balance the excess. Always leave something on your plate and keep portions small. Move away from the table immediately after you finish eating—it's just too easy to nibble if you stay. Keep the right kinds of foods in the house and by all means *don't be afraid to say no.* Keep your goals and the rewards for achieving them in mind constantly and assure yourself that you *can* change—a lot of women have.

Notes

1 Ellington Darden, *Nutrition and Athletic Performance* (Pasadena: Athletic Press, 1976), p. 13.

2 Marie V. Krause and L. Kathleen Mahan, *Food Nutrition and Diet Therapy* (Philadelphia: W. B. Saunders, 1979), p. 19.

3 Ann Lincoln, *Food for Athletes* (Chicago: Contemporary, 1979), p. 1.

4 Nathan J. Smith, *Food for Sport* (Palo Alto: Bull, 1976), p. 3.

5 Frank I. Katch and William D. McArdle, *Nutrition, Weight Control and Exercise* (Boston: Houghton Mifflin, 1977), pp. 17-18.

6 Krause and Mahan, p. 70.

7 Ibid., p. 82.

8 Ibid.

9 Phyllis Sullivan Howe, *Basic Nutrition in Health and Disease* (Philadelphia: W. B. Saunders, 1976), p. 53.

10 Eva D. Wilson, Katherine H. Fisher and Mary E. Fuqua, *Principles of Nutrition* (New York: John Wiley, 1975), p. 39.

11 Jean Mayer, *Health* (New York: D. Van Nostrand, 1974), p. 120.

12 Howe, p. 40.

13 Nutrition Search, Inc., *Nutrition Almanac* (New York: McGraw-Hill, 1975), p. 8.

14 Eleanor Noss Whitney and Eva May Nunnelley Hamilton, *Understanding Nutrition* (St. Paul: West, 1977), p. 59.

15 Wilson, Fisher and Fuqua, p. 60.

16 Howe, p. 88.

17 Katch and McArdle, p. 27.

18 Jean Mayer, "Megavitamine Madness," *Family Health*, February 1980, pp. 48-49.

19 Ibid.

20 Ibid.

21 Katch and McArdle, p. 27.

22 Whitney and Hamilton, p. 371.

23 Krause and Mahan, p. 201.

24 Ibid., p. 203.

25 Whitney and Hamilton, p. 48.

26 Corrine H. Robinson, *Basic Nutrition and Diet Therapy* (New York: Macmillan, 1980), p. 65.

27 Ibid.

28 Lincoln, p. 192.

29 Ibid.

30 Krause and Mahan, p. 48.

31 Howe, p. 37.

32 Whitney and Hamilton, p. 47.

33 Ibid., p. 104.

34 Consumer's Union, "Vegetarianism," *Consumer Reports*, June 1980, p. 357.

35 Corrine H. Robinson and Marilyn R. Lawler, *Normal and Therapeutic Nutrition* (New York: Macmillan, 1977), p. 226.

36 Consumer's Union, p. 360.

37 Ibid.

38 Robinson, p. 159.

39 Robinson and Lawler, p. 227.

40 Consumer's Union, p. 359.

41 Ibid.

42 Ibid., p. 358.

43 Whitney and Hamilton, p. 109.

44 Katch and McArdle, p. 146.

45 Ibid.

46 Ibid.

CHAPTER 4

Posture:
Slump Now, Pay Later

It isn't what I do, but how I do it.
It isn't what I say, but how I say it.
And how I look when I do and say it.

—MAE WEST

Whether your exercise is for figure or for fitness, you should always exercise the habit of good posture. Posture is the structural basis for your figure and contributes to the proper functioning of several physiological processes within your body. Along with its importance physically, posture reflects your physical personality and how you feel about yourself.

You may already have a general idea of what posture is all about, and may be tempted to dismiss the subject in favor of a more challenging one. We hope you will not, because an explanation of the far-reaching effects posture has on your body is truly impressive.

What is posture?

Posture is a general term referring to the way in which the weight of the body is distributed through its center of gravity. "Good posture" involves aligning the body from head to toe: the distribution of weight must be balanced from front to back and from side to side in order for the body to be in proper alignment. The placement or "alignment" of various parts of the body is critical in maintaining postural balance. Here is the ideal alignment, from the ground up:

1. Feet: Parallel with toes straight ahead. The ankle and foot should meet squarely at right angles, indicating even distribution of weight directly

through the ankle. (Note: check the soles of your shoes, especially the heels, for signs of uneven wear indicating poor distribution of weight.)

2. Knees: Neither flexed (bent) nor hyperextended (locked), but loose and held straight.

3. Seat and abdomen: Hips tucked down and forward, stomach pressed in as when holding a deep breath. This is the basis for straightening curves in the lower back, thus eliminating protruding buttocks and abdomen. Think Thin!

4. Shoulders and chest: Upright yet relaxed, chest and rib cage lifted but not exaggerated by an arch in the back. Develop a constant awareness of holding the torso erect. Don't give in to slouching when standing or sitting. Think Proud!

5. Head and neck: Centered squarely above the shoulders, the head balanced evenly with chin parallel to the floor. Avoid tucking the chin or leaning head forward. Think Tall!

When one of these checkpoints is poorly aligned, weight distribution is unevenly directed to your body's base of support. The result is unnecessary strain on muscles, bones, and joints, greater wear and tear on your body—and fatigue.

The fashion world is partly responsible for the posture problem shown in Figure 4-1. The typical model's stance has the same casual slump. We see and imitate! This causes the back to sway, creating a lumbar curvature of the spine, or "sway back," and weakening of the abdominal muscles. In addition, the shoulders may round forward, pressing in on the chest and rib cage. The ever-present effect of gravity pulling down on your body makes it easy to relax into this slouched position. It is work to stand up straight!

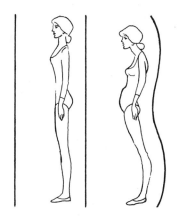

Figure 4-1. Good Posture (left) and the "Fashionable Slump" (right)

Why exercise for posture?

The structural support for body alignment is provided by your skeletal framework. Muscles do the work of keeping your weight balanced and maintaining structural alignment. Your muscles, however, are creatures of habit. If they are not conditioned to work, they become lazy and weak. Opposing groups of muscles (muscles on the opposite sides of the body or limbs) compensate each other; if one group weakens, the other group grows overly strong and pulls the figure out of alignment. For example, when the abdominal muscles are relaxed, the back muscles tighten, causing a hollow back. To correct the imbalance between two groups of muscles on opposite sides of your body, you must choose strength exercises to bring weak muscles back into shape and flexibility exercises to stretch muscles that are pulling the figure out of alignment. In the example described, the abdominals could be strengthened with sit-ups and the back muscles stretched with the pretzel exercise.

A posture inventory

Good posture is a personal achievement and demands a continuous effort which only *you* can give. The first step in establishing good posture is to take your own posture inventory in front of a mirror. From both a front and a side view, check how you normally stand and note the position of the posture checkpoints. Now assume the correct posture shown in Figure 4-1 and make a mental note of the adjustments that you must make between your everyday posture and the correct posture.

The next step is to put your thoughts and feelings to work on improvement. This means acquiring a constant awareness of how you are sitting and standing, then constant practice improving your posture and eliminating poor habits. You may be able to correct some bad habits just by becoming aware of them; for instance, uneven weight distribution of the feet, locking the knees, or jutting the chin forward. Other corrections will take more time and specific exercises. Some exercises are included at the end of this chapter designed to assist in improving posture. These exercises should be supplemented by the flexibility and strength exercises offered in chapters 9 and 7. Concentrate on exercises that will strengthen the abdominals, lower back, and buttocks and stretch the Achilles tendons, calves, front of the hip joint, and lower back.

Posture and your figure

Good posture is part of making the most of what you have and enhancing the natural proportions of your figure. Figure bulges, bumps, and lumps are often caused by incorrect sitting and standing. Remember, form follows function! If you are overweight, you will call less attention to your size and shape if you carry yourself with the poise of good body alignment. Incorrect posture is never a cover-up for figure problems, and may even accentuate the flaws.

You will be convinced of the relationship between your posture and your figure if you will try this simple experiment. All you need is a tape measure. Allow your abdominal muscles to relax and your pelvis to roll forward. Your shoulders and head wil naturally move forward into a slouched position. Measure your bustline, waist, and hips. Now straighten up into good posture: tuck under the hips, pull in the abdominals, lift the rib cage and shoulders. Now measure again and compare the dimensions. This is one of the tricks used by some exercise salons which guarantee a loss of inches in "just one visit." You are distracted from thinking about your posture when they measure you *before* this treatment and reminded to "stand up straight and tall" when measured at the end of the visit.

Posture physiology

Good posture means aligning the skeletal framework to lessen the friction of bone against bone. However, it is not only bones that are involved; shortened muscles may also rub against each other, causing muscular aches and pains.

Back pain, for example, is commonly associated with the muscular imbalance of poor posture. When the muscles extending the length of the spine are strained from constant pulling, you may experience pain in the shoulder and neck as well as in the back. Even headaches can be caused by shortened muscles in the back. Low back pain is frequently caused by shortened muscles in the backs of the legs. The high heels on today's shoes are a major cause of this trouble. The lifted position of the heel constantly puts the calf in a slightly contracted position; when the shoes are removed and the heel is flat on the floor, your calf is actually stretching. Muscle strain may continue up the leg to the lower back.

When the vertebrae in the spinal column are pulled into a curve by overly strong back muscles, an uneven distribution of stress on the individual vertebra results. With time, the uneven wearing of bones caused by stress on the spinal column may cause the pinching of a nerve or even a slipped disc, which could send you to a hospital for corrective surgery. This sort of expense and discomfort can almost always be avoided by working to correct your postural alignment before it becomes a problem.

Next, you should realize that a weakened abdominal wall is partially responsible for most back problems. As postural muscles, the abdominals assist in keeping the back straight, but they have many additional functions of equal importance. They hold the internal organs in place, they support digestive functioning, and they assist the muscles with which breathing is accomplished. These physiological processes, so important to all physical functioning, are less efficient when the abdominal muscles are weak.

As a woman who may someday carry and bear children, you should understand the importance of a straight back and strong abdominal muscles during pregnancy. A straight back enables a woman to carry her baby, both before and after childbirth, with less strain. The environment in which you carry your unborn child is more secure and protected when it is held close in to your body. Delivery will be more natural and safe. And regaining your figure after childbirth will be easier if abdominal muscles are in good shape *before* pregnancy.

The physical personality you project to others comes across in various ways, and the physical presence and poise of good posture is one of them. Poise projects a positive-thinking individual who shows self-confidence. A well-balanced figure reflects the sort of self-respect and pride that are attractive in any situation. Good posture is established by making its practice as habitual as breathing. Don't make excuses for not getting started. The benefits to be enjoyed from the habit of good posture are too close at hand.

Posture exercises

1. Knee Tuck

(lower back and hip flexor stretch)

Lie on back with back flat against the floor. Pull the left knee to the chest with both arms and press tightly to the chest, keeping the right leg flat to the floor. Hold for three seconds. Repeat with opposite leg. Repeat complete exercise five times.

2. Achilles Stretch

(calf and heel cord stretch)

Stand facing a wall with feet two to three feet from the wall. Place the palms of the hands against the wall at shoulder height. Flex the elbows, keep the body in a straight line and feet flat on the floor and touch the nose to the wall.

3. Sitting Long Stretch

(hamstring stretch)

(See chapter 9, p. 89.)

4. Gravity Hang

(See chapter 6, p. 43.)

5. Pop Up

(abdominal strength)

(See chapter 7, p. 50.)

6. Hip Lift

(See chapter 7. p. 56.)

7. Wall Press

Stand with back to a doorway. Place heels about four inches from the frame. Press the small of the back against the frame. Tighten stomach and buttocks, allowing knees to bend slightly, then press neck against doorway. Raise arms to shoulder height and press both hands against the opposite side of the doorway so that the lower back is pressed against the door frame. Straighten both knees. Hold for three seconds. Repeat ten times.[1]

Notes

1 Jack Galub, *The U.S. Air Force Academy Fitness Program for Women* (Englewood Cliffs: Prentice-Hall, 1979), p. 86.

CHAPTER 5

Exercise:
How It Works

Inactivity is one of the great
indignities of life. Through inactivity
people lose their self-respect, their
integrity.

—JOAN CRAWFORD

Another secret to figure control is movement — but it must be the right kind of movement. Exercise is movement designed to maintain, change, and improve our bodies. The study of the human body and the ways in which it responds to exercise is a complex branch of science and much too technical to cover in this book. For those who are interested in gaining a more thorough knowledge, a list of books is recommended at the end of this chapter. This chapter answers some basic questions about exercise in order to provide you with a general understanding of the physiology of it.

Why is exercise important?

Your body is a readily adaptable organism. During the natural processes of growth and aging, it is constantly changing, either developing or deteriorating, in relationship to the physical demands with which it must cope. When no physical demands are made upon your body, its potential and ability to function decline. Chances are that your daily routine does not demand much of you physically. In order to maintain your physical efficiency you must *create* a demand on your system; this can be done through some planned form of physical activity or exercise. Indirectly, exercise is a stimulus for all the functions of your body. It keeps body processes operating efficiently and smoothly, which is a large part of staying healthy.

Why is exercise so important to figure control?

There are two major reasons. First, exercise helps burn the calories that would otherwise be stored as fat, so it can be a significant factor in controlling your weight. Second, and more directly, exercise is responsible for giving you shape because it shapes, tones, and contours your muscles, and muscles are what give shape to your body.

Is all exercise the same?

Definitely not! Exercise is specific and there are three basic categories: (1) *Muscular strength and muscular endurance exercises*. These give you your shape because they strengthen and tone your muscles — which is why we call them "figure exercises." These exercises are fully explained in chapter 7. (2) *Flexibility exercises*. These stretch and lengthen your muscles and enable you to maintain a full range of movement in the joints as you age — which is why we call this the "youth exercise." Chapter 9 contains a full explanation of flexibility exercise. (3) *Cardiovascular endurance exercise*. This is probably the most important of the three types because it is the only one that really works on the heart muscle — which is why we call it the "life exercise." See chapter 8 for a full explanation of this kind of exercise.

Is it important to do all three types of exercise?

Definitely so! A good figure is not worth much if you are not alive to enjoy it. And by the same token, if you allow yourself to become inflexible as you age, you will not enjoy living nearly as much as you should. You want to create a *whole* individual, not one that is put together in parts.

What insures improvement in exercise?

You will respond specifically to the amount and the kinds of exercise you take part in. The key to improvement is to increase the intensity of the exercise by repeating it a greater number of times, or for a longer period of time, or using a greater workload. There are two terms which explain this. The first is *overload*, which means, very simply, an increase in the intensity of the exercise each time you do it. It applies to each of the three types of exercise. To overload a strength exercise, you repeat it more often or increase the resistance to it. To overload a flexibility exercise, you hold the position longer. To overload an endurance exercise, you keep doing it longer or at greater speed. The second term is *progression*; it is simply the consistent application of the overload principle. It means having a plan and sticking with it. It means also to continue your exercises if you expect to improve.

What is meant by muscle contraction and muscle tone?

A contraction can be a shortening, lengthening, or constant static position of a muscle, depending on which exercises are being performed. You contract your muscles when you do strength exercises, and this is essentially what causes you to develop muscle tone. Muscle tone simply means muscle firmness.

What type of exercise will improve the figure?

Exercises which strengthen your muscles are also those which shape and contour your figure. When muscles contract against a force or resistance, they will be strengthened. You may be pushing or pulling, or lifting an object, a body part, or a weight. If you are moving during the exercise, it is an *isotonic* exercise. If you are not moving but your muscles are contracting, the exercise is *isometric* in nature. Isotonic exercise has the advantage of being longer-lasting; with isometric exercise, results are seen more quickly. Because isometrics can be done in a confined space, they are good to use when you are on the job, or when you need to be inconspicuous. However, you should remember that isometrics burn far fewer calories than exercises which involve bodily movement; and there is no way they can give you a perfect figure in "six minutes a day."

Why are muscles important to the figure?

Muscles are the underlying tissues in your body which are alternately contracting and relaxing to make you move. As we have said, muscular contraction will contour and tone the muscles. In short, muscles are what give your figure shape; a shapely muscle means a shapely you! The condition or shape of the muscle, not the size, is determined by its use. Muscles that are not used will waste away or *atrophy*. An atrophied muscle appears loose and flabby.

Will exercise build bulky muscles or produce a masculine appearance?

This is an important question because the fear of becoming larger and "masculine" has kept many women from exercising. Exercise affects only the condition of the muscle, *not* the size. The size of your muscles is determined by factors such as heredity, hormones, weight, and sex. As a woman, you need never worry about building large, bulging muscles because the hormones that govern your muscular structure are very different from a man's. Structurally, a woman has fewer fibers within each muscle than a man has, which also means that she has less potential for strength development. Each muscle is made up of thousands of these tiny, hair-like fibers, which can support up to a thousand times their own weight! Hence, if compared with a man, a woman of equal size and weight and with the same history of physical activity would not be as strong.

The predominantly male hormone testosterone plays a major role in determining the mass and bulkiness of muscles. In women this hormone is present, but in such small amounts that it has virtually no effect on muscle size. Testosterone, like other anabolic steroids, has been produced synthetically and has been taken by some athletes to stimulate development of muscle mass and strength. Another biological difference is that a woman has a thicker layer of fat deposited around her muscles, which gives her a softer appearance and feel. Men's muscles are more sharply defined and firmer. Chemically, the elements within each sex's muscles differ, although the significance of this has not yet been fully explained.

How do muscles work?

Muscles require oxygen, which is supplied by the blood, in order to contract. Contraction requires energy and produces heat which helps to maintain body temperature. This is why you feel warm when you begin to exercise, and why movement keeps you warm when it is cold outside. Muscles work in pairs, one flexing or bending a joint and the other extending or straightening it.

Will flexibility exercises contour the figure?

Stretching exercises are for flexibility; they won't do much toward shaping your figure. They are important to your mobility, because flexibility keeps your movement free and unrestricted. When it is easy for you to move, you are more likely to keep moving. When your movement is stiff and restricted, you are more likely to curtail your movement.

What is meant by the "stretch reflex"?

Your muscles will automatically react against being stretched. Tiny receptors are located in the muscles to keep them from over-stretching and to aid in posture control. Sudden stretching stimulates several receptors at once, leading to an exaggerated contraction. This does not occur when the stretch is made gradually. This is why we do not recommend ballistic, or bouncing, stretching movements. Using a repeated bounce to achieve flexibility is not as effective because of the stretch reflex. Also if the stretch reflex should "let go" as you are bouncing, you may overpull and tear muscle fibers. For this reason, ballistic stretch movements are more likely to cause soreness.

What is a "static stretch" exercise?

Static means non-moving, and stretch means to lengthen or pull. Therefore, static stretch refers to an exercise involving a stretching movement where you gradually pull into the position and hold without moving for a minimum length of 15 seconds to a maximum hold of one minute.

What causes inflexibility?

When your muscles are constantly contracted during normal activity and exercise, the muscles and tendons shorten. If there is a lack of regular movement for a length of time, the range of movement of the joints is inhibited. Muscles become tight and more susceptible to injury, especially tearing and pulling, when joints are inflexible. A good example is one who has just had an elbow cast removed: it will be difficult, if not impossible, to straighten the arm right away if the cast has been on for several weeks.

Will exercise alone promote weight loss?

Weight loss is possible by increasing your caloric expenditure through exercise while your caloric consumption remains the same, but it is a very slow process which can be most discouraging. Therefore, as stated in chapter 3, most excess weight should be removed through diet and food control. Exercise should be used as an aid to losing and redistributing weight.

Why do muscles cramp during exercise?

They are simply telling you they are lazy and they don't like the exercise. Cramps often occur when you are not used to the activity, and they are nothing to worry about. To relieve the cramped muscle gently stretch the affected muscle and hold in a static stretch until the cramp subsides, then continue exercising. It is not necessary to stop exercising every time you encounter a muscle cramp because cramps do not indicate muscle damage.

Will exercise change fat into muscle?

Absolutely not! Fatty tissue and muscular tissue are not the same thing and are not interchangeable. Your chances of converting fat into muscle are about the same as learning to see with your ears.

Is it normal to experience a weight gain when beginning an exercise program?

Yes, but only temporarily. In most cases, the gain is due to fluid retention caused by the soreness of your muscles. Also remember that muscle tissue weighs more than fat but *consumes less space.*

Is it normal to feel tired and sore after exercise?

Yes, it is very normal to experience tiredness, soreness, and pain, especially in the beginning. New demands are being placed on the body, causing temporary fatigue that will disappear when the body adjusts to the new schedule of exercise. The more sedentary and unaccustomed to exercise you have been, the more soreness and pain you will probably experience. Do not become discouraged and discontinue your exercise program but pace your work in the beginning by slowly increasing your workload. Muscular soreness can be diminished if you warm up properly before exercise and end your exercise program with static stretching. Relief from the soreness that often occurs the day after exercise is helped by warm baths and light stretching exercise.

Is it possible to spot reduce?

No. Evidence shows that spot reducing is a claim, not a fact. Basically, our heredity determines the distribution of fat deposits on our bodies, and also how and when those fat deposits will be used. This is why each of us loses and gains weight differently. We all have our problem areas.

Are there exercises that accomplish more than one purpose?

Yes. Many endurance activities, for example, will involve the large muscle groups of the body, helping to shape them and your figure, while also working on your cardiovascular system; in addition, they will burn many calories, thus promoting weight loss. A few exercises will combine strength and flexibility. For example, the knee-to-nose sit-up (chapter 7, p. 51) will shape the hip, thigh, and abdominals and will also stretch the muscles in the back of the leg. The waist twist (chapter 7, p. 55) will contour the torso and provide flexibility in the upper back. These combination exercises are particularly good ones to do because of their double benefits.

Will strength or flexibility exercise benefit the heart?

Unfortunately, not much. The heart itself is a specialized type of muscle and it is extremely important that you exercise it properly. Exercise for the cardio-vascular system is called endurance exercise, but don't confuse cardiovascular endurance with muscular endurance. Muscular endurance refers to a par-ticular muscle's ability to repeat a movement several times, and it is closely related to a muscle's strength capacity; cardiovascular endurance comes from exercise that strengthens the heart.

Are there exercises to relieve mental or emotional tension?

Yes, very specific ones! Tension from the stresses of everyday living can wind up as tension and fatigue within your body. First, you must learn to control this build up of tension by identifying the cause. Then you can work toward releasing the tension. We must learn to put our conscious process of relaxation to work on controlling the release of tension. A good outlet for tension is regular recreational activity, re-"creating" a store of strength for mind and emotions. Relaxation will be discussed at length in chapter 10.

Is it possible to feel rejuvenated after exercise?

Very definitely. This feeling of rejuvenation is common, especially after the first few weeks of exercise. The support systems of your body are stimulated by exercise. Your metabolism increases as well. The heart delivers increased amounts of blood throughout the body and, in exchange, the circulatory system eliminates waste more quickly. The result is unexpected; you feel like you have more energy instead of less!

What effects will time and aging have?

In order to maintain strength and muscle tone, and for weight control, exer-cise will continue to be a significant factor in your life. Not only does metabolism decrease with age, making it more difficult to maintain your desired weight, but the number of active cells in the body will decrease also. This means the body spends energy supporting inefficient tissue. Weight con-trol becomes increasingly important for the continued health and well-being of your body. The less active we become, the more limited our range of move-ment is. Flexibility is maintained only through the proper movements. Since injury and healing become more serious with age, the preventive factor of maintaining flexibility becomes more valuable. The deteriorating effects of time are compounded by the normal tendency to become more sedentary. Establishing exercise as a regular habit early in life will help you to maintain your health and body to a greater degree and for a longer time.

How will exercise affect pregnancy?

Many physicians are finding advantages in a good exercise program during pregnancy since there are increased physiological demands on the body during this period. In fact, research has shown that women athletes have shorter labors, fewer Caesarian sections, fewer backaches, and fewer complications during pregnancy than nonathletes. The intensity of your exercise program should be dependent on how active you were before pregnancy. Use common sense and consult with your physician to determine any limitations you should place on your physical activities and exercises.

What is important in planning an exercise program?

There is no magic formula for figure control that works for everyone. However, we can offer a few realistic guidelines that can be individually adjusted, and some suggestions that may be useful in establishing goals.

1. *Keep an up-to-date record of your weight.* You should measure weight daily. Weigh at approximately the same time of day, preferably the first thing in the morning. Weigh without any clothes on. A record of your weight will create an awareness of weight increases before they become major problems.

2. *Keep a weekly record of your measurements.* Changes in your weight without concurrent changes in proportion indicate that you are not getting the exercise you need to complement your weight control program. Use the same tape measure each time.

3. *Record your food intake daily and tally calories at the end of each day.* Remember, in order to lose weight you must take in fewer calories than you expend through activity. Determine the average number of calories you are taking in and the major sources for any extra calories over and above your needs.

4. *Determine the number of calories you use in a normal day.* Use the Energy Expenditure Chart (Appendix B) to keep a record of your total calorie expenditure. In order to maintain your present weight, this expenditure must match each day's calorie intake. In order to lose weight, the calorie expenditure must be greater than the calorie intake.

5. *Determine a regular program of exercise.* To complete your figure program, the rest of your efforts must go into a regular program of exercise. Your program should include a balance of exercises from each of the chapters on exercise.

6. *Keep a record of your exercises.* A record of the intensity, duration, and repetitions of each exercise will give you a basis for evaluating your progress and the effectiveness of your program. Your current physical condition will determine the starting point for your exercises. Choose exercises which you can do and repeat them until it becomes a real effort to do any more. When you find that it is becoming easier to complete the exercise, you must either make the exercise more strenuous or choose a more difficult exercise. As your body adjusts, improvement will continue only if you progressively increase the exercise load.

7. *Evaluate your exercise program constantly.* In the beginning stages, improvement will occur rapidly. It becomes more difficult to continue the rate of improvement as you progress. Constant evaluation and change will help overcome the plateaus of slow improvement. Once your goals have been met, overload is no longer your guiding principle. Exercises should continue to be done regularly, but on a more diversified basis. To maintain your level of conditioning, it becomes important to maintain your level of interest. Therefore, it is recommended that *regular exercise* supplement various physical activities which are strenuous enough to give your body vigorous activity.

How often is exercise needed?

This, of course, depends on the type of exercise you are doing and its purpose. If you are working toward improvement, exercise must be done daily. You will begin to lose the effects of your exercise in approximately two days of no exercise. Thus, a minimum program must plan for exercise at least every other day. The key to exercise is that it be done regularly, with a minimum of three times per week.

What is the best time of day to exercise?

There is no particular time of day which is best for exercising, but there is one time to avoid, if possible. This is the time directly following your meals. When you are digesting foods, the blood supply to the digestive tract is increased. When vigorous activity is imposed on your system, it also requires increased amounts of blood to be sent to the major muscle groups involved in exercise. Both demands for blood cannot easily be met at the same time, so it is best that you wait for at least one hour after eating before you exercise.

How about a weight chart?

Finding a realistic guide for today's ideal slender figure is no easy task. The charts most commonly used are generally based on averages, and the average person in America today is overweight. Therefore, most weight charts are not based on "ideal figures." You will find an "ideal figure" weight chart in Appendix A to this book. The data on this chart accurately reflect the figure most sought after by today's woman.

A final note

Now you are ready to set some realistic goals for yourself. While taking into account your time schedule and eating habits, give thought to establishing new habits for healthy living. Once you have begun a program of exercise, stick with it—and keep your goals in mind.

Suggested Readings

Per-Olof Astrand and Kaare Rodahl, *Textbook of Work Physiology* (New York: McGraw-Hill, 1977).

Herbert A. deVries, *Physiology of Exercise* (Dubuque: Wm. C. Brown, 1976).

Donald K. Mathews and Edward L. Fox, *The Physiological Basis of Physical Education and Athletics* (Philadelphia: W. B. Saunders, 1976).

Jack H. Wilmore, *Athletic Training and Physical Fitness* (Boston: Allyn and Bacon, 1977).

CHAPTER 6

Warm Up and Warm Down

Even as airplane engines must be
tuned up before taking off, so must a
human being have a tuning up process. The body has many miles of
blood vessels and nerves to stimulate, if you want to travel in high gear.

—NORMAN VINCENT PEALE

Warm up

Warming up your body to prepare for more strenuous exercise is vitally important in the prevention of muscular injury and severe muscle soreness. In
order to warm up the muscles properly, begin your exercise program gradually with the light stretching exercises described in this chapter. Slowly increase the pace and intensity of the exercise until your body begins to feel loose
and warm. Perspiration is an excellent indication that your muscles are indeed
warm and ready to endure more intense exercise. Since each person is at a different level of fitness, the amount of time spent warming up will vary with
each person. Some persons will need at least fifteen minutes of warm up;
others will require more time; and a few can get by on less.

Perspiration is a good indication of your readiness to take on more
strenuous exercise. Perspiration occurs when your normal body temperature
rises because of the increase in blood and muscle temperatures. This increase
is important in order to prepare your muscles properly so that you are less
likely to sustain injury or severe soreness. Because the flexibility, endurance,
and strength exercises place considerable stress on the muscles, the importance
of a warm up cannot be emphasized enough.

Aside from the prevention of severe muscle soreness and injury, a thorough
warm up brings other benefits. For instance, since the blood and muscle

temperatures have been increased, the functioning of muscles improves, and this will enable you to benefit more from your exercise. Also, the processes which help burn calories are increased during a warm up, and the burning of calories is what you want in weight loss.

Warm down

You would not stop an automobile by running it at seventy miles an hour into a brick wall; instead, you anticipate and begin braking gradually until you come to a complete halt. By the same token you should warm down the body in the same way that you warm up, with a gradual change in the tempo of activity. By using light stretching exercise you will begin to slow the pace naturally, allowing the body to cool off.

During vigorous activity the muscles assist the circulation of blood. If all activity stops abruptly the effect could be a pooling of blood in the extremities, which might result in muscle cramps or sudden blacking out.[1] This is why it is just as important to include a warm down in your exercise program as it is to include a warm up. One suggestion for a good ending: sitting down, slowly rotate your head around, rotate from side to side, and finally just let your head hang forward. Now would be a good time for your relaxation (see chapter 10).

Warm up and warm down exercises

Begin your warm up slowly. Do not select a warm up exercise more vigorous than the activity you are preparing to undertake. Jumping rope, which is an excellent endurance exercise, would be too intense an exercise to begin with. Start with light stretching exercises to insure against muscle injury and soreness. Many of the flexibility exercises can be used in warm up and warm down by lightly stretching (see chapter 9). You can then incorporate some light jogging, running in place, or skipping if you do not feel adequately warm.

Hints
1. Remember to concentrate on warming up the whole body and not just a portion of it.
2. On cold days, warm clothing should be worn during the warm up period and removed before activity since this helps increase muscle temperature.
3. No more than a few minutes should pass between warm up and activity or the warm up benefits will begin to diminish.
4. Do not warm up to the point of fatigue.

The following are examples of the types of exercise that can be used for light stretching when warming up or warming down:

1. Side Bend
(See chapter 7, p. 54. Use the same exercise with light stretching.)

2. Standing Waist Twist
(See chapter 7, p. 55. Use the same exercise with light stretching.)

3. Overhead Stretch
Standing, feet together, hands and arms overhead. Reach with one hand as high as possible as if to touch a star. Reach slowly with other hand. Repeat total exercise several times.

4. Toe Touch
Standing, feet together. Bend forward from the waist and try to touch toes with hands. Repeat slowly several times.

5. Gravity Hang
Standing, feet shoulder-width apart. Bend forward from the waist and hang. Pretend you are a rag doll. The force of gravity pulls the upper body down. You should feel a pull in the back of your legs.

6. Sitting Long Stretch
(See chapter 9, p. 89. Use the same exercise with light stretching.)

7. Wide Stride Stretch
(See chapter 9, p. 89. Use the same exercise with light stretching.)

Note

1 Herbert A. deVries, *Physiology of Exercise* (Dubuque Iowa,: Wm. C. Brown, 1976), p. 138.

CHAPTER 7

The Figure Exercise: Strength

Health and fitness are better than any
gold, and bodily vigour than
boundless prosperity.

—ECCLESIASTICUS XXX:15
(*The Apocrypha*)

Muscular strength refers to the ability to exert force or overcome resistance. The muscles must contract to push, pull, lift, or work against resistance. This is what strength exercises are all about—working your muscles against resistance and therefore firming, tightening, and contouring them. Just as men perform strength-building exercises to develop their bodies, you will find that the same strength-building exercises will contour your female figure.

The two types of resistance exercises are isometrics and isotonics. Using one of these types of strength exercises, or a combination of the two, increases the strength of the muscle. Pushing, pulling, or lifting a resistance is called isotonic exercise. An example of an isotonic exercise would be a push up, since the muscles involved have to push or lift the weight of the body; the body is acting as the resistance. Isometric exercises involve working against an immovable or controlled resistance; such a resistance could be created by pushing both hands together with equal force, therefore contracting the muscles, and holding the exercise until the muscles begin to quiver.

Currently, the best form of resistance exercise is weight training, which in most cases is isotonic exercise because you are pushing, lifting, or pulling a resistance. Machines have revolutionized the field of weight training. Some are designed to adjust constantly to the muscle contraction of the user and to give optimal resistance whatever the angle of pull. Weight training is an excellent form of strength exercise because if offers a quick and easy way to overload the muscles. (Over-load was discussed in chapter 5.) In order to develop greater strength, which is also the key to contouring, muscles must be challenged to work against a greater resistance once they have become adjusted to a particular load.

Since most persons do not have easy access to complex weight training equipment, the strength exercises in the first part of this chapter are ones that use the body's own weight as the primary resistance; thus they can be performed easily at home. However, if you wish to purchase ankle, wrist, and waist weight belts to supplement your strength program it will bring results more quickly. (The ankle, wrist, and waist weight belts do not reduce those specific areas, of course; their purpose is to add load to the limb or total body, and thus increase the work of the muscles.) Many other items found in the home can be used as weights, such as large books, canned goods, ski boots, heavy wrenches, irons, pots and pans, or plastic bleach bottles filled with sand.

Developing a program

As you begin to develop a strength exercise program it is important to maintain a balance of exercises. Even though you may feel that one particular part

Exercise	Number of Repetitions								
	Date								
	6/1	6/3	6/5	6/9	6/11				
1. Standing waist twist	25	30	30	36					
2. Arm fling	15	18	20	20					
3. Standing leg lift	16	17	18	19					
4. Side bend	20	24	24	24					
5. Sitting ankle flexion and extension	30	35	36	40					
6. Popups	12	12	13	14					
7. Kneeling leg lift series	10	12	13	13					
8. Letdown	4	7	8	8					

Figure 7-1. Example of a Chart for a Strength Exercise Program

of your body needs more emphasis than another, the key to a good shape is to first balance the exercises for all parts of the body, then add extra exercises for problem areas. This chapter contains many exercises grouped to serve different areas of the body.* Start your program by taking a look at your time schedule and then selecting as many exercises from each body area as your time will allow. List these exercises on a sheet of paper, then make a chart like the one shown in Figure 7-1. You can copy the form shown in Figure 7-2.

Exercise	Number of Repetitions								
	Date								
1. Standing waist twist									
2. Arm fling									
3. Standing leg lift									
4. Side bend									
5. Sitting ankle flexion and extension									
6. Popups									
7. Kneeling leg lift series									
8. Letdown									

Figure 7-2.   A Strength Exercise Program

Repeat each exercise as many times as you can. When each exercise has been completed, record the number of repetitions on the chart. Each time you exercise (work out) try to increase your number of repetitions for each exercise. When your exercises begin to take too much time to perform, add a weight load using one of the items mentioned above. The load will allow you to perform fewer repetitions, thus making your exercise time shorter.

*We shall not recommend any facial contortion exercises, because some cosmetic surgeons argue that such exercises can cause unnecessary wrinkling. It should be noted that exercises for the upper body also exercise the muscles of the face.

Strength Group I

**NECK
SHOULDERS
UPPER ARMS
UPPER BACK**

1 Head Lift

Position: Lie on back with arms at side.

Action: Lift head (only) as high as possible and return to starting position. Repeat at a steady pace.

POSITION AND ACTION

2 Push Up

Position: Assume prone position supported on hands and toes with body absolutely straight. Keep body straight throughout exercise.

Action: Lower body to two to six inches from floor and push back to starting position. Repeat at a steady pace.

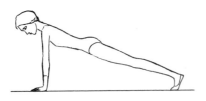

POSITION FOR EXERCISES 2 AND 3   ACTION FOR EXERCISES 2 AND 3

3 Let Down

(An alternate for the push up. To be done until you can push up.)

Position: Same as exercise 2.

Action: Lower body as slowly as possible until you can no longer hold body in horizontal position. Return to starting position any way you can. Repeat.

4 Arm Fling

Position: Stand, feet apart, arms at shoulder level in front of shoulders with elbows bent.

Action: (1) Fling bent elbows as far behind body as possible while keeping arms at shoulder level.
(2) Return to starting position and fling arms straight backward, try to touch hands at shoulder level. Return to (1) and repeat exercise (alternate steps 1 and 2). Use a fast pace.

POSITION   ACTION (1)   ACTION (2)

5   Arm Circles

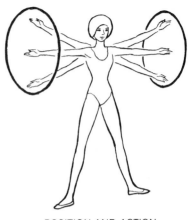

Position: Stand, feet apart, arms extended to sides of body at shoulder level.

Action: (1) Rotate arms forward in a large circular motion. Rotate from large circles to small circles.
(2) Same exercise as (1) with backward rotation. Repeat at steady pace.

POSITION AND ACTION

Strength Group II

**ABDOMINAL MUSCLES
WAISTLINE**

6   Pop Up

Position: Lie on back (supine), knees bent, feet secured,* head raised off floor with chin touching chest, back rounded, arms folded across chest.

Action: Curl the upper body just a few inches off the floor and return to starting position. Use a fast pace.

POSITION AND ACTION

---

*More abdominal benefit will be achieved if the feet are not secured. Therefore, work without your feet secured as soon as possible.

7   Isolated Sit Up

Position: Lie on back (supine),
knees bent, feet up on a chair or
other object that is approximately
20 inches high and allows feet to be
secured. Head should be raised off
floor with chin touching chest, back
rounded, arms folded across the
chest.

Action: Curl the upper body just a
few inches off the floor and return
to starting position. Use a fast pace.

POSITION AND ACTION

8   Knee-to-Nose Sit Up

Position: Lie on back (supine) with arms extended overhead.

Action: Raise leg (leg straight) and at the same time raise upper body to
sitting position. Grasp leg with hands (as close to ankle as possible) and try
to touch knee with nose. No rest between sit ups. Repeat on opposite leg.
Use a steady pace.

POSITION   ACTION

Jack Knife Sit Up

Position: Lie on back (supine) with arms extended overhead.

Action: Raise both legs (legs straight) and at the same time raise upper body to sitting position. Touch toes with fingers while in pike position. Use a steady pace.

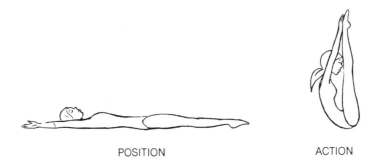

POSITION   ACTION

1O **Wide-Stride Sit Up**

Position: Lie on back (supine) with arms extended overhead and legs in stride position (knees about two feet apart).

Action: (1) Raise torso to sitting position and reach with both arms toward left foot. Lie down. Use a steady pace. (2) Raise torso and reach straight forward between legs. Repeat (1) but reach for right foot.

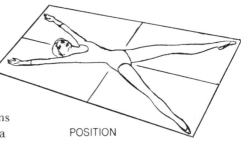

POSITION

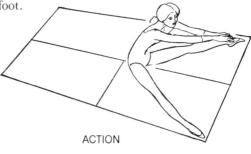

ACTION

11 Scoop *

Position: Sit with knees bent, legs together close to chest, feet off floor, and hands on floor behind body for support.

Action: (1) Extend legs three inches from floor. (2) Lift legs straight up to extended V position. Return to starting position. Repeat at a steady pace. (An alternate position is with upper body resting on elbows throughout exercise. Use this position until you can accomplish the regular position.)

POSITION   ACTION (1)   ACTION (2)

12 V Sit *

Position: Same as extended V position in exercise 11.

Action: Slowly raise and lower legs. Repeat at a steady pace.

POSITION   ACTION

---

*If lower back pain is felt, discontinue the exercise and strengthen the abdominal muscles through another exercise until these exercises can be performed without pain.

13   Twisting Sit Up

Position: Lie on back (supine), knees bent, feet secured,* head up with chin touching chest, back rounded, arms folded across chest.

Action: Use pop up exercise and twist to alternate sides while sitting up. Repeat at a fast pace.

POSITION   ACTION

14   Side Bend

Position: Stand, feet apart, one arm circled overhead and one circled downward in front of body.

Action: Keep body and hips in vertical alignment and bend as far to one side as possible. Exchange arms and repeat movement to other side. Use a fast pace.

POSITION AND ACTION

---

*More abdominal benefit will be achieved if the feet are not secured. Therefore, work without your feet secured as soon as possible.

15 Standing Waist Twist

Position: Stand with legs apart and arms at shoulder level in front of shoulders with elbows bent.

Action: Keep body straight from waist down. Turn upper body (including head) as far as possible to the right, then as far as possible to the left (alternate directions). Arms must be held at shoulder level with elbows bent. Repeat at a fast pace.

POSITION   ACTION

16 Sitting Waist Twist

Position: Sit with legs straight and toes pointed. Support body by placing hands on floor at sides.

Action: Roll from one side to the other (over buttocks). Palms must remain on floor. Repeat at a fast pace. (This is an exercise that has been done incorrectly and has been said to reduce the size of the hips, which is false.)

POSITION   ACTION

Strength Group III

HIPS
LOWER BACK
THIGHS

17 Hip Lift

Position: Lie on back (supine) with knees bent and arms at side.

Action: Lift hips as high as possible, leaving shoulders and feet on floor. Return to starting position. Use a steady pace.

POSITION　　　　　　　ACTION

18 Seat Lift Leg Extension

Position: Assume crab position—body supported on feet and hands, knees bent, seat on floor.

Action: (1) Lift seat. (2) Lift and extend leg. (3) Return leg to floor. (4) Return seat to starting position, and repeat using other leg. Use a steady pace.

POSITION AND ACTION (4)　　ACTIONS (1) AND (3)　　　ACTION (2)

19   Side-Lying Leg Lifts

Position: Lie on side, support body on hands, with arm and upper body straight.

Action: (1) Lift one leg up to side of body; then behind body; then in front of body. Alternate sides by rolling on buttocks and using other leg. Use a steady pace. (2) Hold top leg high, lift bottom leg to meet top leg. Alternate sides. Use a steady pace.

POSITION AND ACTION (1)

POSITION AND ACTION (2)

20   Side-Lying Double Leg Swing

Position: Lie on side, both hands in front of body for support, upper body straight, legs raised off floor, and toes pointed.

Action: Swing both legs in front of body to opposite side in same position. Keep legs straight and off floor through the swinging movement. (Arms must be lifted for legs to pass in front of body.) Repeat at a steady pace.

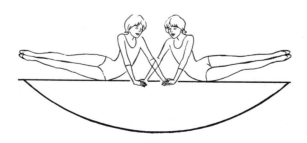

POSITION AND ACTION

21 Swan

Position: Lie prone (face down) with arms and legs extended.

Action: Lift chest, arms, and legs off floor. Hold in upward position. Repeat at a steady pace.

POSITION AND ACTION

22 Kneeling Leg Lift Series

Position: Down on hands and knees.

Action: (1) Extend leg to side, keep leg straight. Touch toe to floor and raise upward as far as possible. Head up. Repeat at a steady pace. (2) Extend leg to rear, lift straight leg, bend knee behind head, and straighten leg again at a steady pace. Keep head up. Repeat. (3) Extend leg to rear, lift leg as high as possible, drop leg down, and bend knee forward, bringing knee to chest and dropping head to meet knee. Repeat at a steady pace.

POSITION

ACTION (1)

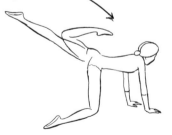

ACTION (2)

ACTION (3)

23 Standing Leg Lifts

Position: Stand resting one hand on back of chair (or similar item) for balance with weight on inside leg (next to chair), knee bent slightly. Outside leg is held slightly behind and to side of body, leg straight and pointed toe resting lightly on floor.

Action: (1) Lift outside leg to the side as high as possible, lower to floor and repeat. Use a steady pace. (2) Lift outside leg to the rear as high as possible, lower to floor and repeat. Use a steady pace. (3) Lift outside leg to the front as high as possible, lower to floor and repeat. Use a steady pace. (Body must remain upright. Use correct posture, with head held high. Use arm position shown. Repeat exercises on both sides of body.)

POSITION AND ACTION (1)

POSITION AND ACTION (2)

POSITION AND ACTION (3)

24 Stride-Leg Crossover

Position: Assume a supine position (lying face up), body extended, resting (off floor) on heels, upper body supported on hands (arms straight) and legs apart.

Action: Cross one leg over the other (legs straight and seat lifted) turning body as you cross. Touch toe as far to one side of body as possible and return to starting position. Repeat on opposite side. Use a steady pace.

POSITION

ACTION

25 Slimmer Bounce

Position: Assume a stride position, with knees bent, feet angled outward, back straight, and arms to side of body at shoulder level.

Action: Lower and raise seat in an up-and-down motion, keeping knees bent at all times. (The feet must be at least two feet apart with knees angled the same as the feet. The knees must remain directly over the feet at all times. The seat must not drop below the knees. The body position is similar to that of sitting in a straight-back chair.)

POSITION

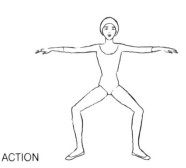

ACTION

Strength Group IV

CALVES
ANKLES

26 Heel Raises

Position: Standing, feet apart, arms to side of body at shoulder level.

Action: Raise heels up as far as possible (on toes). Repeat with feet parallel, angled out, and angled in. Use a slow pace.

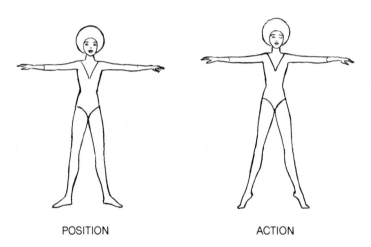

POSITION   ACTION

27 Sitting Ankle Flexion and Extension

Position: Sit with legs straight, support body by placing hands on floor at sides.

Action: Extend toes forward as far as possible, then pull toes back as far as possible. Repeat at a fast pace.

POSITION AND ACTION

Weight training

Women's weight training has become so popular that figure salons, fitness centers, and health clubs designed especially for women are spreading throughout the country. Women are realizing the many benefits of training with weights—specifically, that this is the most efficient way to contour the figure. The fears that weights will cause bulging muscles and loss of femininity are beginning to diminish as more information is available to the contrary.

The commercial salons and clubs offer pleasant surroundings, attractive weight training equipment, swimming pools, and saunas and can help motivate you to go regularly, work out, and relax. Many have excellent programs and instruction; unfortunately, just like in any other business, there are those that the consumer should beware of. Watch for salons and clubs that have vibrating machines and rollers, which can have damaging effects (see chapter 2), instead of sound, proven equipment. Examples of well-known equipment are Universal Gym and Nautilus, both of which are usually supplemented with a variety of free weights (barbells and dumbbells). These pieces of equipment make *you* do the work rather than the equipment doing it to you. Just as some salons offer good programs and instruction, some are staffed with individuals who have little or no knowledge of physiology and weight training. So if you are going to place your hard-earned cash on the line, do some investigating before joining. Buyer beware!

The following paragraphs provide essential information and exercises necessary in starting a weight training program. Most of the equipment described is inexpensive and may be found at local schools and gyms.

The system to use   For all practical purposes, the simple "set system" of weight training is the most effective method for you. A set consists of a certain number of repetitions of a single exercise; in a simple set system, all of the sets of a given exercise are performed before moving on to the next exercise. For example, two sets of eight repetitions means that you do a given exercise eight times, rest for about one minute, and then do the same exercise again eight times. Repetitions should be performed without interruption, using a pace not too fast and not too slow.

A graduated program   There are many types of weight training programs. With proper supervision, a program can be individualized and made much more technical. The graduated program described here is a basic one—effective and simple to follow.

Program I:	One set, 15 to 20 repetitions
Program II:	Two sets, 10 to 15 repetitions
Program III:	Three sets, 5 to 10 repetitions

Follow Program I for approximately six weeks, working out three times a week and using the resistance progression described below. Then begin Program II and complete the same procedure before moving on to Program III.

Resistance progression Resistance refers to the load or the amount of weight being used in an exercise. The proper load for each individual differs for each exercise, since some persons are naturally stronger than others. The simplest method of determining the correct resistance for each exercise is old-fashioned trial and error. Just pick a weight you think you can handle without much strain. If you can't use it to complete the number of assigned sets and repetitions of an exercise, it's too heavy. The next time you work out, select a weight that seems light enough to permit you to complete the exercise. Make a chart like the one shown in Figure 7-3 and keep a record of the changes made in your program. You can copy the form shown in Figure 7-4.

Muscles will adjust to a certain load, so it is necessary to increase the resistance after you can easily complete the designated number of sets and repetitions of an exercise. Remember, here you do not increase the number of repetitions or sets; increase the resistance instead. This overload is vital in achieving the greater strength required for figure contouring.

Number of exercises Every program should include exercises for each area of the body. An ideal program will include at least 10 to 15 exercises, with more

Program ___I___	Sets ___One___		Repetitions ___15___							
Exercise	For	Changes								
		Date								
		6/15	6/17	6/19	6/21	6/23	6/25	6/27	6/29	6/31
1. Arm Curls	Arms	10lbs.	10lbs.	10lbs.	12lbs.	12lbs.	15lbs.	15lbs.	15lbs.	20lbs.
2.										
3.										
4.										
5.										
6.										
7.										
8.										

Figure 7-3 Example of a Chart for a Progressive Resistance Program

Program _____	Sets _____	Repetitions _____											
		Changes											
Exercise	For	Date											
1.													
2.													
3.													
4.													
5.													
6.													
7.													
8.													

Figure 7-4   A Progressive Resistance Program

exercises to be added for problem areas. In order to minimize fatigue, avoid doing consecutive exercises for the same part of the body. The length of time to spend on a workout depends on the number of exercises in your program. A good workout will take from one to two hours.

Performing the exercise   Correct posture is important, regardless of the exercise position. For example, when standing keep your body straight and your feet about a shoulder-width apart, with your knees unlocked; when sitting keep your shoulders directly over your hips; when lying down on your back, pull your abdomen in and try to hold your back flat against the bench. During all exercises, don't forget to breathe regularly. The two most common grips, and the ones that will be used for the following exercises, are the over grip and under grip, as shown in Figure 7-5.

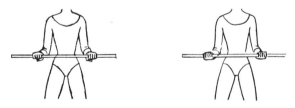

Figure 7-5. Overgrip (left) and Undergrip (right)

Weight Training Group I

NECK
SHOULDERS
UPPER ARMS
UPPER BACK
CHEST
SIDES

1   Wrist Curls, *undergrip*

Rest forearms on thighs
and flex wrists upward
as far as possible.

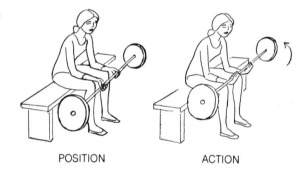

POSITION   ACTION

2   Arm Curls, *undergrip*

With arms fully extended
bend arms bringing
weight to chest.

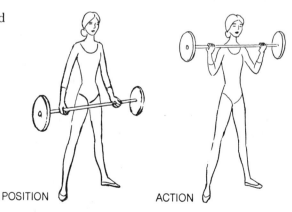

POSITION   ACTION

3 **Triceps Press,** *overgrip*

With arms extended overhead, lower bar as close to the back of the head as possible.

 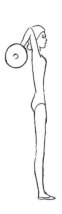

POSITION   ACTION

4 **Rowing,** *overgrip*

With hands close together bring bar upward to chin keeping elbows high.

 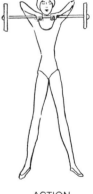

POSITION   ACTION

5 **Supine Lateral Raises,** *undergrip*

Raise arms upward above chest with arms extended.

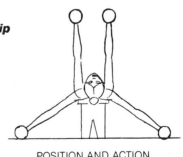

POSITION AND ACTION

Bench Press, *overgrip*

Support bar over chest and extend
arms upward.

POSITION

ACTION

 Overhead Press, *overgrip*

Lift bar overhead until arms
are fully extended.

POSITION   ACTION

Prone Lateral Raises, *overgrip*

Bring arms upward as far as possible.

POSITION AND ACTION

Weight Training Group II

ABDOMINAL MUSCLES
WAISTLINE

 Sit Up

The higher the elevation of the
incline board, the more difficult the
sit up.

POSITION AND ACTION

10 **Dumbbell Side Bend,** *overgrip*

Bend to one side as far as possible
and then to the other side. Keep
feet together.

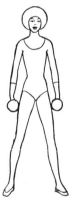 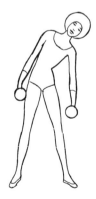

POSITION   ACTION

11 Barbell Waist Twist, *overgrip* *

With barbell resting on shoulders, turn upper body as far in one direction
as possible. Alternate directions. As a safety precaution use care with
heavier weight.

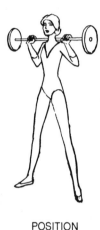 

POSITION   ACTION

12 Barbell Side Bend, *overgrip* *

With barbell resting on shoulders,
bend as far to one side as possible
and then to the other. Be careful
with heavier weights.

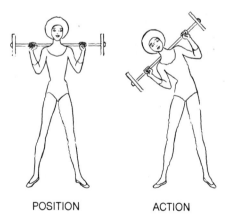

POSITION   ACTION

---

*Individuals with back problems might want to use alternate exercises.

13   Leg Raises, *ankle weights*

With arms overhead
grasping end of board,
bring knees to chest,
extend legs upward
and lower.

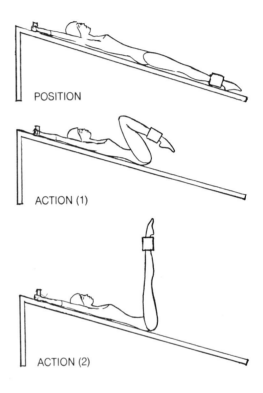

POSITION

ACTION (1)

ACTION (2)

14   Hip Flexor, *overgrip*

Hanging from a horizontal
bar, bring knees up to chest,
using ankle weights.

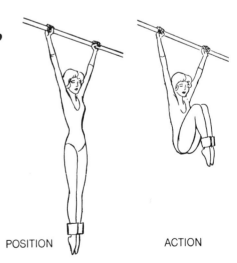

POSITION   ACTION

Weight Training Group III

HIPS
LOWER BACK
THIGHS
CALVES
ANKLES

15 Deadlift, *overgrip*

Lift bar and assume a standing
position.

POSITION

ACTION

16 Hack Lift, *overgrip*

Lift bar and assume a standing
position.

POSITION

ACTION

17   Leg Raises, *side, rear, and front, with ankle weights*

Standing erect, raise leg upward as far as possible. Do not kick leg. Do each position as a separate exercise.

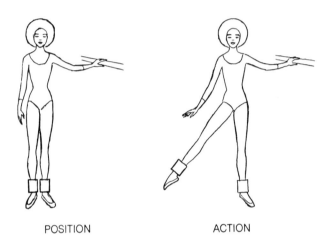

POSITION   ACTION

18   Heel Raises, *overgrip*

With bar resting on shoulders, raise heels off floor as far as possible. Do in three positions: with toes pointed inward, outward, and parallel.

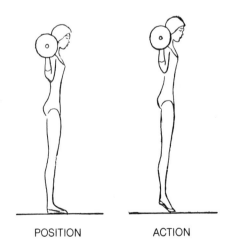

POSITION   ACTION

19 One-Half Squat, *overgrip*

With bar resting on shoulders, squat as if sitting on the edge of a chair.

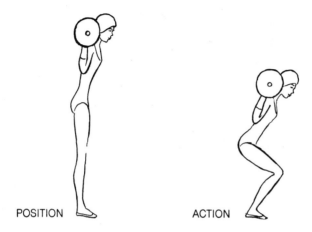

POSITION   ACTION

20 Standing Forward Bend, *overgrip**

With bar resting on shoulders, bend forward keeping back straight.

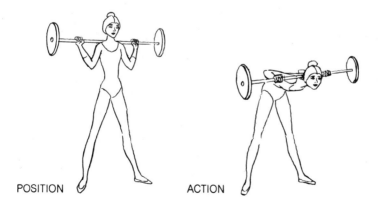

POSITION   ACTION

*Individuals with back problems might want to use alternate exercises.

CHAPTER 8

The Life Exercise: Endurance

May you live all the days of your life!
—JONATHAN SWIFT

All human activity is fundamentally dependent upon the production of energy by the body.[1] The systems of the body most important to this process are the circulatory and respiratory systems, and the one most important organ is the heart. These are the truly vital mechanisms of the body because all of life's processes depend on them.

The heart must pump nutrients, oxygen, and waste products to and from the organs and tissues of the body through a complex network of arteries, veins, and capillaries while at the same time helping other vital organs perform their functions. Oxygen and waste products are received and eliminated through the respiratory system. If these systems fail, the entire organism fails.

The ability to remain healthy and to meet the demands of the living environment is directly related to the state of efficiency of the *cardiorespiratory system*, the term used to describe the heart, circulatory, and respiratory systems.[2] Research has shown that the amount and type of physical activity has a close relationship to the state of efficiency of the cardiorespiratory system.

Environmental effects

As more labor-saving devices are invented and placed into use, the average person's life style becomes more sedentary. The ordinary day in earlier generations included a great deal more physical activity than the present does. This was of necessity, of course. Now, however, instead of needing rest after a work day, most people need a good, strenuous exercise session!

Research studies have indicated that inadequate physical activity increases the risk of coronary heart disease.[3] In one longitudinal study, the number of heart attacks for sedentary men was double that of active men. Inactivity is also a precursor of obesity, and obesity has been linked to heart disease.

There is a close relationship then between inactivity, obesity, and heart disease. It is interesting to note that athletes, who continue to be active throughout life, have a below-average risk of heart attack.[4] If people are compared on the basis of degree of exertion, the least active tend to have the greatest degenerative disease and health rates, with quality of health and life span increasing in direct proportion to increased physical activity.[5]

Activity can be controlled by adding the right type of exercise to our lives. Although it cannot be said to cure all ills, exercise clearly helps prevent many diseases, including heart disease. By restructuring our life styles to include proper nutrition, the control of body weight, and a cardiorespiratory conditioning plan, it is possible that future generations might see coronary heart disease diminished as a critical health problem.[6]

Factors important to successful programs

The three factors most important to success in planning a cardiorespiratory endurance program are the *frequency*, *duration*, and *intensity* of the exercise session—in other words, how often do you exercise, for how long, and how vigorous or strenuous was the exercise session?

The number of times (frequency) you workout each week is not as important a consideration as the other two factors.[7] Three to four workouts a week are sufficient. Keep in mind that more frequent workouts will allow you to reach your goals more quickly; however, you will experience success with the fewer number of workouts—it will just take a little longer. The length (duration) of each workout or exercise session is *very* important. However, the one most critical factor is the intensity of the exercise session. Although research has shown that a workout of only five to ten minutes duration results in improvement, the suggested length of time for best results is twenty to thirty minutes.[8]

The intensity level at which you work out will be the real indicator of your success. In addition, the intensity of the workout must increase as you get used to activity. This, remember, is called *overload*. Recent studies have shown that a high degree of success may be obtained by a series of short, very intense workouts with short rest periods in between.[9] This is contrary to past beliefs.

A successful method of combining both duration and intensity is to alternate from periods of heavy intensity to periods of lighter intensity throughout the workout while working out for a longer duration.[10] An example would be a run-walk-run program. Another successful method is to work out at moderate intensity continuously for a longer period of time. All methods will result in improvement of cardiorespiratory endurance, provided they are continued on a regular basis.

Monitoring the intensity of the workout

Sophisticated laboratory methods exist for monitoring the intensity of a workout, such as using an electrocardiogram while running on a treadmill. However, these are much too impractical for the average individual. Using your own pulse rate is the most practical method. In order to use this method effectively, you need to know that there are three pulse rates: the resting pulse rate, the active pulse rate, and the recovery pulse rate.

The resting pulse rate is an indication of your normal heartbeat; it is the pulse rate taken after you have been sitting quietly for at least ten minutes. An effective cardiorespiratory endurance exercise program will result in a lowered resting pulse rate. This is an indication that your heart and cardiorespiratory system are becoming stronger and can accomplish their work within your body with less effort. When your resting pulse rate begins to decrease, you will know that your exercise program is working. For example, Roger Bannister, the first man recorded to have run a mile in less than four minutes, lowered his resting pulse rate from the high seventies to the low forties. It is not uncommon for a marathon runner to have a resting pulse rate in the thirties.

The active pulse rate, which is taken during the workout, is an indication of the intensity of the exercise. In order to lower the resting pulse rate, you must overload the cardiorespiratory system during the exercise session, as discussed earlier. This will result in an increased pulse rate during the active phase of your workout. Therefore, you should monitor it at various intervals during your activity. Take a few moments to stop and count your pulse, then continue your exercise. The program you select will indicate your use of this pulse rate.

The recovery pulse rate is very important as a guide to whether your workout has been too strenuous. It should be taken approximately thirty minutes after finishing your exercise session and should be taken in the same manner as the resting pulse (after you have been sitting quietly for at least ten minutes). This pulse count should be very close to your resting pulse count. If it is still high (roughly, more than five beats higher than your resting pulse), your workout has been too strenuous for your level of physical fitness, and you should reduce the intensity of your workout at the next exercise session.

Counting your pulse is best accomplished by using the arteries on either side of the neck. This is called the carotid pulse and is located to the side of the Adam's apple where the neck joins the head. The pulse may also be taken at the wrist where it is located below and on the thumb side. The pulse must be taken by the *fingers*, not the thumb, in order to be read accurately. Use the second hand of a watch or clock to count the number of beats in fifteen seconds, then multiply by four and you will have your number of heartbeats per minute.

Cardiorespiratory exercise programs

Although strength and flexibility exercises have specific benefits for the muscles and joints of the body, they do very little to stimulate the heart, circulatory, and respiratory systems. The type of activity that best does this is cardiorespiratory endurance exercise. This exercise stimulates the cardiorespiratory system, resulting in an increased pulse rate during the activity, causing perspiration and heavy breathing, and in general invigorating the entire body.

Activities conducive to cardiorespiratory endurance conditioning include walking (vigorous), jogging and all types of running, swimming, bicycling, roller skating (vigorous), aerobics, bench stepping and stair climbing, rope jumping, hiking, and mountain climbing. Although most of the activities listed will fit the requirements of the cardiovascular endurance programs given in this chapter, the focus here will be on walking, jogging, and running programs. These three activities can be performed almost anywhere, anytime, anyplace. They are convenient, require no special facilities, need very little extra clothing, and are activities that nearly everyone is able to perform.

Cardiorespiratory programs are designed around the factors discussed earlier. Hopefully, they will meet the needs of most runners except perhaps the very advanced or competitive runner. Keep in mind that illness, especially bed rest, may alter an achieved level of improvement to some extent.[14] So don't expect to get up out of the sick bed and begin where you left off. You may have to drop back to an earlier level in your exercise program or even to a different program — one of lesser intensity if your bed rest was sustained for a long period of time. If this should happen, make the necessary adjustments, begin again, and build back up to your original level. Then you can go forward again.

The Maximum Pulse Rate (MPR) system   The maximum pulse rate (MPR) system is for the beginning runner. It is based on the principle that as an individual engages in cardiorespiratory exercise, the heart rate increases in direct proportion to the intensity of the exercise and at some point reaches a peak or plateau.[15] This point is called the *maximum heart rate*. Research has shown that there is a gradual decline in the maximum heart rate with age.[16] Authorities[17] use the following formula to approximate an individual's maximum heart rate.

$$\text{HR Max} = 220 - \text{Age} (- \text{ or } +) 10 \text{ beats}$$

This formula plus former research studies have been combined to design a beginning exercise program which lists a predetermined maximum heart rate (based on age) that an individual should attempt to reach during a workout.[18] Since the pulse is used to indicate the heart rate, it is called the maximum pulse rate, or MPR, system. The set rates are shown in Table 8-1.

Table 8-1   MPR (by age)

Age	MPR
10–19	180
20–29	170
30–39	160
40–49	150
50–59	140
60–69	130
70 +	120

This system will allow you to begin a running exercise program safely and teaches you to establish the habit of taking your pulse during exercise. In addition, it gives you a point at which to end your program. Many beginners simply do not know when to stop. The idea is to continue activity until you have reached your MPR; however, don't attempt to reach it the first time out. Instead, work to increase your pulse rate gradually until you are able to work to your maximum pulse rate. In the beginning, end your workout when you are tired and record your active pulse rate at that point. Later you will be able to continue and end your program when your MPR is reached.

The walk (don't run) system   The walk system is another program helpful for the beginner and those who cannot run because of physical problems. The entire system is based on walking. Chart a distance of one mile and break it into quarters. If you are really out of shape, begin with half a mile. If you begin with half a mile, attempt to walk the distance in twenty minutes and continue until you walk one mile in thirty minutes. You should eventually be able to walk three miles in forty-five minutes. When you can walk one mile in thirty minutes, aim for one and a quarter miles in the same amount of time, then one and a half miles, and so on. When you can walk two miles in thirty minutes, change the workout time to forty-five minutes and attempt two and one quarter miles. Strive to build up to three miles in forty-five minutes. Of course, you can continue to add miles and time, keeping in mind that the goal is always a fifteen-minute mile.

Walk-run systems   There are a number of variations of walk-run programs, but all combine a walking rest period with running. One such program is based on time and requires no charted distance. Another program uses an oval track and requires no stopwatch. A third program is a good system for working into a running program.

The *timed program* is based on seven intervals of running and walking, which are divided into levels, as shown in Table 8-2.

Table 8-2   The Timed Walk-Run System

Level One: 14 minutes		*Level Two: 21 minutes*		*Level Three: 28 minutes*	
Run	2 minutes	Run	3 minutes	Run	4 minutes
Walk	2 minutes	Walk	3 minutes	Walk	4 minutes
Run	2 minutes	Run	3 minutes	Run	4 minutes
Walk	2 minutes	Walk	3 minutes	Walk	4 minutes
Run	2 minutes	Run	3 minutes	Run	4 minutes
Walk	2 minutes	Walk	3 minutes	Walk	4 minutes
Run	2 minutes	Run	3 minutes	Run	4 minutes

Level Four: 32 minutes		*Level Five: 36 minutes*		*Level Six: 37 minutes*	
Run	5 minutes	Run	6 minutes	Run	7 minutes
Walk	4 minutes	Walk	4 minutes	Walk	3 minutes
Run	5 minutes	Run	6 minutes	Run	7 minutes
Walk	4 minutes	Walk	4 minutes	Walk	3 minutes
Run	5 minutes	Run	6 minutes	Run	7 minutes
Walk	4 minutes	Walk	4 minutes	Walk	3 minutes
Run	5 minutes	Run	6 minutes	Run	7 minutes

Spend one to two weeks at each level, or progress at your own speed if you find moving to the next level too difficult. Levels 1 and 2 are, more or less, introductory in that they prepare your body in stages for more intense work. Level 3 is the first level that begins to meet criteria for real cardiorespiratory improvement. Running programs where the activity lasts for at least three minutes and is followed by light activity for an equal or lesser amount of time result in aerobic or cardiorespiratory improvement.[19] You may want to remain on levels 4, 5, and 6 for longer periods of time. Move to the next level when it is comfortable for you and remain as long as you feel that you are gaining benefit from that level of exercise.

The *distance program* is based on a quarter-mile track. Many individuals find they need the structure of a very definite distance in order to work out successfully. Set your first goal at *one mile*. Run the sides and walk the ends of the track oval four times. Move toward running the complete oval one time and walking the next time for four times. When you can do this, you are ready for the next step. Your next goal will be *two miles*. Continue to run one quarter and walk the next for the first mile and add the second mile by beginning it the same as the first (running the sides and walking the ends). Work toward running one quarter and walking one quarter for the second mile until you are alternating running one quarter with walking one quarter for eight quarters (two miles). Set your goal now at three miles and add the third mile in the same manner. This amount of exercise should provide some cardiorespiratory benefit. Progress at your own speed as time allows. A variation of this program is to remain at the three-mile mark while striving toward running two quarters and walking one quarter, then repeating this for three miles. This can be continued until you are running the first mile, walking the second mile, and running the third mile.

A *transitional program* bridges the gap between running and walking. The ultimate goal is to run the entire distance. This program can be a progression from the distance program, or it can be started by charting a distance in advance. Select a distance that best fits the amount of time you can or want to spend in exercise. The exercise times listed in Table 8-3 are based on a ten- to fifteen-minute mile, which most people should be able to achieve even with a run-walk.

Table 8-3   Exercise Times (by distance)

Distance	Time
5 miles	60–75 minutes
4 miles	40–60 minutes
3 miles	30–45 minutes
2 miles	20–30 minutes

You should complete your charted distance each time you work out. Start with running and walking while attempting to run more of the distance with each exercise session until you can run the entire distance. Then work on your running time until you can achieve or go below the minimum time listed for your charted distance.

Training for serious running   When you can run continuously for three miles or more, you are ready for a more sophisticated running program. There are probably as many running systems as there are serious runners. Your program will depend on your goals and the objectives you wish to achieve through running.

If you are running for the exercise benefit only, then a four- to five-mile continuous running program should be sufficient. If, however, you are tempted to consider competition running, such as marathon or mini-marathon running, you will want to establish a training program that improves both your speed and distance.

The *serious or competition runner* usually trains a minimum of six days a week; sometimes twice daily. The workout should vary from long, slow runs of various distances to interval training.

The rule of thumb for long, slow distance runs is to go 25 to 50 percent farther than the distance at which you are going to compete.[20] For example, if a ten-kilometer (approximately six and two tenths miles) race is your goal, run between seven and one half and nine miles each workout.

Interval training is designed to improve speed and is similar to the run-walk program. You might want to alternate running quarter- and half-mile intervals. For example, on the first day, run six quarter-mile intervals while timing your pace. In the beginning, walk a quarter mile between each interval. Work toward jogging between intervals. For your second speed workout, run four half-mile intervals for time and walk or jog a quarter mile between each interval. These are merely examples. Your intervals might be shorter or longer, depending on your goal. When the intervals become easy, add to the number of intervals you are running. As you improve, increase the distance of your intervals.

One workout day should be spent running the distance of your competition race for time. In addition, you might want to include a sprint workout by running back-to-back 100's. Run 100 yards at a sprint pace and, with no more than 30 seconds rest, run 100 yards again. Begin with ten such sequences and work up.

As mentioned previously, there are many different methods of training. The ideas here are only to help you get started. They are not an attempt to delve deeply into race-running techniques. Many books have been written on this subject, and additional reading will help you establish your own training schedule.

Suggestions prior to beginning your program

You should warm up prior to your workout with light stretching and walking, as suggested in chapter 6. Your workout should also end with a warm down, as suggested. Increase the duration and intensity of your workout gradually. Following are nine mistakes listed by *Runner's World* magazine as common in beginning runners.[11]

1. *Don't go too far, too fast, too soon.* Overstress and overconditioning lead to injury. Beginning runners expect improvement to occur too quickly. Be patient and improve naturally.

2. *Don't ignore pain.* The beginning runner will feel some discomfort at the start of a program until the body adjusts. However, extreme pain or pain that does not go away with rest should not be ignored. The exercise is too intense if you are dangerously out of breath. Runners can develop serious injuries if they ignore pain; it is not true that you should be out of breath when you run. Mild discomfort during the exercise session, which leaves when the workout is concluded, can be overlooked. Extreme pain must be dealt with!

3. *Honestly evaluate your level of physical fitness before you start.* Even though you were previously an athlete, you are not necessarily physically fit unless you have stayed active. If you have no illness or past history of heart disease, you should be able to work into a program gradually with no undue effect. Individuals with a past history of major disease or a family history of heart or metabolic disease should seek the approval of their doctor before beginning a running program.

4. *Don't skip a proper warm up and warm down.* As stated previously, this is an important area—one that is all too often neglected or passed over. Warm up adequately and stretch out after your workout. For warming up you might try running very slowly while taking short strides until your body begins to feel warm. In addition to gradually slowing down after running, be sure to include a liberal number of stretching exercises.

5. *Use proper equipment.* Proper shoes are very important. The number of running shoes on the market today is astounding. Your choice should be a shoe of good quality. Quality, in this case, is on a parallel with cost. The more expensive shoe will not necessarily last longer but is designed to support your foot better while running and is less apt to cause blisters and other foot problems. People who begin a running program should make sure they buy running shoes and not merely shoes that look like running shoes.[12]

There are a number of excellent running shoes available, none of which are inexpensive. Probably the best way to begin to make a selection is to ask friends and acquaintances what shoes they like best. Then go to a good *athletic shoe store* and try on shoes until you find a pair that feels good. It is probably best to buy more than one pair if you can afford to, or another pair as soon as you can. Since feet sweat while running, alternating shoes will allow them to dry out between workout sessions.[13] In addition, shoes are designed according to the type of surface on which they are to be used and for different training situations. Make certain that you purchase an appropriate pair or pairs for the surfaces and situations for which you will be using them. Clothes should be *loose* and comfortable. Select a lightweight sweat suit for cool days and one a little heavier for cold days. In addition, on cold days you will need gloves and something to cover your head and ears.

6. *Choose a comfortable running style suited to your body.* Beginners should use short, shuffling strides; most start out with high, long strides which cause premature fatigue and possible injury. The foot action is not actually heel, midfoot, toe. Persons with high arches will tend to strike more toward the ball of the foot first, while those with lower arches will end to hit the ground more flat footed. This is fine. Running should be done in a relaxed manner. The tendency is to tense the upper body, head, neck, arms, and hands in the initial stages. You will have to think consciously about relaxing these areas in the beginning. Keep your hands open and loose. Shake them periodially while running to keep them loose.

7. *Don't ignore the terrain.* In the beginning, select simple and easy locations for running. Don't try hills until you are well into a running program. Beginners are often found on terrain too difficult for them and sometimes on terrain too difficult for experienced runners. Knee injuries and stress to the Achilles tendon are often the result of hill running by the inexperienced runner. Try to stay off concrete and asphalt as much as possible. These surfaces are hard and can cause undue soreness and even joint injury to the beginning runner who may not be making contact with the surface correctly.

8. *Avoid an improper diet.* This book includes an entire chapter on diet because its importance cannot be overestimated. The body functions best on a balanced diet. When you use energy, you will want to make certain that the energy you take in, in the way of food, is the energy that allows the body to best meet its needs. It is probably best not to eat within three hours of a running workout. In fact, most faithful runners like to run on a completely empty stomach which can easily be the case if the workout is early in the morning. Don't forget the importance of water and other fluids. Consume them prior and even during your workout, especially if it is hot weather.

9. *Don't quit because of minor injury.* Don't give up easily; minor injuries always occur. In the beginning, when you may be running improperly, injuries can occur because of improper contact of the feet with the running surface. Heel bruises, Achilles tendon overstretch, muscular soreness, and joint aches and pains are all common to the beginner. See a doctor if the pain is severe; otherwise, adjust your running style and your exercise session accordingly. Remember: Don't be a victim of *over run.* Repeated mistakes are costly and can lead to serious injury. Try not to make them, and you will probably continue long enough to become an experienced runner.

Breathing

Much has been said about breathing and breath control while running. Many competitive runners breathe in through the nose and expel the breath forcefully through an open mouth. Their breathing is paced along with their stride. The beginner, however, need not be concerned with breathing except to remember to breathe. Many times, beginners become tense and tend to hold their breath. This causes even more tension. *Think natural!*

A final note

The importance and benefits of cardiovascular exercise cannot be over-emphasized. Remember that it is the type of exercise that probably uses the most calories, and it is the one type of exercise that you must not neglect. You should engage in a cardiorespiratory workout on a regular basis.

It is more fun to work out when you work out with others, so try to get a group together. The biggest problem with this type of exercise is motivation. When you exercise in groups, you can urge each other on and make the exercise a game. It is also unwise for beginners to run or bicycle alone, and in many areas it is just not a good practice for anyone. Therefore, for safety's sake, do activities in pairs or groups.

If you are going to attempt hills and more advanced types of terrain, it is best to learn the proper techniques. Classes in running are available through county agencies, public schools, colleges and universities, the YMCA and YWCA, and through private agencies. Take advantage of them and learn the correct form.

Finally, it is wise to have a complete physical examination before engaging in a cardiorespiratory exercise program. Remember to start out slowly and not to overdo in the beginning. Expect to be somewhat sore for the first two weeks, but let your soreness be a gauge for the intensity of your program. Don't be surprised if your endurance exercise program becomes your favorite hobby!

Notes

1 John L. Place, *Health* (Englewood Cliffs: Prentice-Hall, 1976), p. 281.

2 James J. Burd and Leonard T. Serfustini, *Quest One Active Living: A Guide to Fitness, Conditioning and Health* (Dubuque: Kendall/Hunt, 1978), p. 29.

3 Jack H. Wilmore, *Athletic Training and Physical Fitness* (Boston: Allyn and Bacon, 1977), p. 201.

4 Charles A. Bucher, Einar A. Olsen and Carl E. Willgoose, *The Foundations of Health* (Englewood Cliffs: Prentice-Hall, 1976), p. 226.

5 *Essentials of Life and Health* (New York: Random House, 1977), p. 196.

6 Burd and Serfustini, p. 40.

7 Wilmore, p. 209.

8 Ibid.

9 Per-Olof Astrand and Kaare Rodahl, *Textbook of Work Physiology* (New York: McGraw-Hill, 1977), pp. 398–401.

10 Ibid., pp. 404–405.

11 Steven Subotnick, "9 Mistakes Runner's Make," *Runner's World*, April 1980, p. 72.

12 Hal Higdon, *Beginner's Running Guide* (Mountain View: World, 1978), p. 90.

13 Ibid., p. 93.

14 Arthur J. Vander, James H. Sherman and Dorothy S. Luciano, *Human Physiology: The Mechanisms of Body Function* (New York: McGraw-Hill, 1980), p. 363.

15 Wilmore, p. 32–33.

16 Astrand and Rodahl, p. 189.

17 Wilmore, p. 33.

18 Astrand and Rodahl, p. 354.

19 Ibid., p. 404–413.

20 Higdon, p. 204.

CHAPTER 9

The Youth Exercise: Flexibility

I shall grow old but never lose life's zest,
Because the road's last turn will be the best.

—HENRY VAN DYKE

Flexibility is the quality of being pliant, versatile, and adaptable to change. Flexibility exercise is called the *youth exercise* because it combats the effects of aging on the range of movement of body joints. With age, our bodies tend to become restricted in the actions of bending, stretching, and reaching which came easily in youth. If we were to return to the school playground and attempt to go through the motions of the past, most of us would be unable to perform the antics and movements of our youth. This is indication enough of our loss of flexibility.

Flexibility exercises are designed to alleviate inflexibility caused by shortened muscles and ligaments as discussed in chapter 5. Flexibility exercises stretch the muscles that need stretching, allowing us to have more freedom in our movement and enabling us to work more efficiently. This freedom to move, to reach and bend without restriction, will also provide a feeling of youthfulness, which many of us feel we have lost, and an appearance of youthfulness as well. If we feel young physically and mentally, we can approach aging with a more positive outlook.

Many of the aches and pains associated with old age are caused simply by inflexibility in the joints. Muscles drawn so tightly that they ache can soon become a source of chronic pain. Flexibility exercises, by eliminating the source of the problem, can ease many of our aches and pains. Furthermore, if our joints are flexible, many strains and sprains can be avoided; in this respect, flexibility exercises help prevent serious injury.

General information about flexibility exercises

Care should be taken before beginning the exercises included in this chapter, so read and heed the following information.

Warm up   Since flexibility exercises place great stress on the muscles, it is extremely important that you take an adequate warm up before your workout. Try to spend at least ten minutes warming up before attempting a static stretch position.

Static stretch   Two common techniques are used in flexibility exercise: the dynamic stretch and the static stretch. The first method is not recommended. It is called dynamic or ballistic stretching because it involves bouncing, bobbing, and jerky movements. The dynamic method stimulates the stretch reflex, which was discussed in chapter 5, and inhibits the stretching of the muscle that needs to be made flexible. In addition, it often causes unnecessarily severe muscle soreness.[1] The best method for increasing flexibility is static stretching, which involves holding muscle groups in a stretched position for a recommended period of time. This method counteracts the stretch reflex and allows for relaxation of the muscle fibers.[2]

Number of days and duration   Your flexibility program should be followed at least five days per week to attain optimum success. If time permits, go through your program once in the morning and again in the evening. Once you have reached your desired level of flexibility, you can cut your program down to three times a week.

To achieve the best results from flexibility exercise, try to hold each position for fifteen seconds. As you progress, work up to thirty seconds, forty-five seconds, and to a maximum of one minute. Since it is not feasible to use a stopwatch while exercising, count one, one thousand, and so on instead. Remember to work both on time and on achieving the proper position for each exercise and variation.

Positions   As you begin the exercises described in this chapter, most of you at first will not be able to achieve many of the positions shown. In every such case, begin with whatever position your level of flexibility will allow, and each time you exercise attempt to come closer and closer to the prescribed position. Remember not to bounce in order to achieve a position; instead, pull slowly and hold each position without moving. Mastering both the position and the maximum hold will take time, so be patient. You will find that some exercises will be easier than others. Don't cheat yourself by eliminating a difficult exercise from your program.

Exercises

Hips One of our most common problems is inflexibility of the hip joint, which makes it difficult to achieve the correct position in the sitting exercises. Generally, most people cannot angle the hips forward while in a sitting position and if these exercises are done incorrectly they will be of little benefit. For example, in the sitting long stretch we usually sit with the hips tilted backward, the back rounded, and the head down as shown in Figure 9-1(a). To correct this assume the position in Figure 9-1(b) by keeping the back absolutely straight, the chin up, and most important, the hips angled forward. One

a. Incorrect   **b. Correct**

Figure 9-1. The Sitting Stretch

of the best ways to correct this common occurrence is to think "belly button down, head up." Concentrate on angling the hips forward, keeping a straight, almost arched, back with your chin and your head up while keeping your eyes fixed on a spot or object in front of you. The minute you allow the hips to tilt backward, while rounding the back, you lose the benefit of the exercise.

Notes

1 Herbert A. deVries, *Physiology of Exercise* (Dubuque: Wm. C. Brown, 1976), p. 437.

2 Ibid., p. 434.

Flexibility Group I

HIPS

1 Sitting Long Stretch

Position: Sit with legs together and straight, keep back straight, hips tilted forward with hands grasping ankles.

Action: (1) With feet pointed, pull body forward while keeping chin up and neck stretched. Attempt to touch your belly button to your thighs. Hold position. (2) Repeat same exercise with feet flexed.

 POSITION

 ACTION

2 Wide-Stride Stretch

Position: Sit with legs apart, hips tilted forward, and back straight. Determining how far apart the legs should be depends upon each individual's level of flexibility. If the knees bend during the exercise the legs are too far apart. Work to widen the stride as you progress.

Action: (1) With feet pointed, grasp as far down one leg as possible, pull body forward while keeping chin up and neck stretched. Attempt to touch your belly button to your thigh. Repeat to the front with one hand grasping each ankle. Then repeat action on the other leg. (2) Repeat same three actions with feet flexed.

 POSITION

 ACTION (1)

 ACTION (2)

3 Frog Stretch

Position: Sit with knees bent outward and soles of feet together. With elbows out grasp feet while keeping chin up, hips forward and back straight. In the maximum position the knees should be flat on the floor with the heels of the feet touching the crotch.

Action: Pull body forward with chin up and neck stretched. Attempt to touch your belly button to your feet.

POSITION   ACTION

4 Standing Bend or Stretch

Position (1). Stand with feet slightly apart, knees bent and hands on floor in front of toes. The distance between the hands and feet will vary depending on your flexibility. The more flexible you are, the closer the hands will be to the feet.

Action (1). Straighten legs and hold position without bending knees. When this position can be held for maximum time, move on to position 2.

Position (2). Stand with knees bent, grasping ankles behind heels with elbows behind knees.

Action (2). Straighten legs and hold. Try to pull chest to knees.

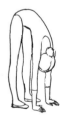

POSITION (1)   ACTION (1)

POSITION (2)   ACTION (2)

Flexibility Group II

BACK

5 **Pretzel**

Position: Lie on back with arms at side.

Action: Raise legs overhead until balls of the feet are resting on the floor as close to the head as possible while keeping legs straight. Do not let the knees bend. As you progress, move the feet closer to the head.

ACTION

6 **Prone Arch**

Position: Lie prone (face down) with hands on floor directly beneath chest.

Action: Lift upper body with arms, bend legs at knee while pointing feet toward head. Arch back attempting to bring feet and head as close together as possible. Keep thighs and pelvis on the floor.

ACTION

7 Back Arch

Position: Lie on back with arms overhead, elbows bent, and hands on floor. Bend knees with feet on floor close to seat.

Action: Lift body while extending elbows and knees, arch back, and tilt head back. Work toward achieving a high back arch and moving hands and feet closer together. It might be wise to have a partner help lift you the first few times.

ACTION

Flexibility Group III

SHOULDERS
ANKLES

 8 Shoulder Stretch

Position: Stand clasping hands behind back with arms straight.

Action: (1) Raise arms as high as possible without leaning forward. Keep a straight vertical position. As you progress, have a partner raise your arms higher, because it will be impossible, after a point, for you to do so on your own. (2) Bend forward at the hips and bring clasped hands overhead. The force of gravity will aid in pulling the arms downward.

POSITION   ACTION

Ankle Stretch

Position: Stand resting weight on
one foot; roll opposite foot forward
and over so that full sole is exposed,
then carefully apply weight to the
top of the foot.

Action: Gradually place more and
more weight on the foot. Repeat on
opposite foot.

POSITION AND ACTION

CHAPTER 10

The Sanity Exercise: Relaxation

Go placidly among the noise and
haste and remember what peace
there may be in silence.
—MAX ERHMANN

The relationship of the mind and body has been mentioned throughout the book. In no other exercise do they work together as closely as in the conscious process of relaxation. Relaxation is time given to renew and refresh our strengths—physical, mental, and emotional. We call relaxation the sanity exercise because of the calming effect it has on our lives. No matter what life brings, we are able to face it with less fatigue, and evaluate the consequences of our actions with better judgment, when our minds are relaxed and decisions are not made in haste. When we feel physically and mentally tired, we operate less efficiently, and consequently live with insecurity, worry, tension, and anxiety. These circumstances, continued over a period of time, may manifest themselves in several ways—difficulty in falling asleep or getting restful sleep, moodiness, depression, and ultimately mental and emotional breakdown.

Recent evidence shows that a large percentage of physical and emotional disorders are directly linked to life changes and stressful events. One standard medical text estimates that 50 to 80 percent of all diseases have their origins in stress.[1] Stress is defined by Hans Selye as "the nonspecific response of the body to any demand made upon it."[2] The body's ability to adapt to situations—be they pleasant and positive or unpleasant and negative—is the stress reaction. The physiology of the body's response to stress is as follows: "The body responds—or attempts to respond—to any type of stress in the same manner. Interpreting the stress as a call for action, it mobilizes itself through the interaction of the nervous and glandular systems which control the level of body activity. Adrenalin is secreted, stored energy is released, blood sugar level rises, and heart rate and blood pressure increases. When the stress is removed, calming hormones are released, and the body returns to normal."[3]

Tension has been singled out by the American Medical Association as a major cause of heart attacks. Tension is the sensation and emotion you feel as a result of continuous mental and emotional stress, theoretically in response to a physical or psychological threat. *Muscular tension is always an accompanying symptom of general tension.* Using electromyography, we can measure the response of muscle to various kinds of stress. The next time you sense a feeling of pressure, indecisiveness, excitement, anger, or frustration, notice the tightness in your muscles.

Perhaps one of the most damaging influences on well-being is negative thinking. An imagined situation may evoke almost the same emotional response as a real one. When you dwell on imaginary problems or anticipate trouble of some sort, you create a threat to your well-being. Our bodies grow tense with anxiety and emotion. By turning from negative to positive thoughts, you take charge of your emotional responses and save energy for productive and pleasant situations.

Exercising your powers of relaxation has become necessary to offset the fast pace of living and the pressures of time. The psychological difficulty in keeping up with the changing values and patterns of living takes its toll in well-being. Techniques used to handle stress include Jacobsen's progressive relaxation, autogenic training, breathing exercise, yoga postures, acupressure or shiatsu finger manipulations, movement experiences and responses such as regular aerobic training, T'ai Chi, Aikido, or similar vigorous exercise or activity programs.

The following exercises and techniques for relaxation and handling stress are provided in the hope that they will be practiced with real effort and concentration.

Relaxation exercises

The following are exercises to use when you have the advantage of solitude, and a quiet place for a retreat. Music will help promote relaxation if it is soothing and quiet. Do not let your emotions or thought processes interfere with physical relaxation. Particularly in the beginning, the most important point of concentration should be your body.

1. Choose a particular time of day and make an effort to sit quietly for a few minutes each day at that time.

2. Sitting in a cross-legged position, rest your hands in your lap or on your knees. Gently close your eyes and concentrate on a single thing. Choose something that is pleasing for you to think about. Each time your mind is distracted, bring it back to your object of concentration.

3. Sitting quietly with your eyes closed, tighten your fists and mentally explore the feeling of tension within your hands. Slowly release the hands, studying the feeling of relaxation. Practice this several times until you are able to identify relaxation as it happens. Try this with different parts of your body.

4. Find a comfortable position lying on the floor. Try lying on your back, your head turned to one side, your arms away from your body, your feet and ankles loose. Turn your palms up and tighten your hands into a fist. Slowly let your hands relax. Concentrate on the feeling of relaxing your hands. Send the release up through your arms and relax the entire body.

5. Lying on the floor, roll to one side and curl up, bringing your knees to your chest. This is a position familiar to us as children. Turn your thoughts back to the day when you were young and life was full of adventure and curiosity. As you return to the present, bring back with you that sense of wonder and open your eyes to the adventures that lie ahead.

6. Find a position of relaxation. As you slowly close your eyes to the visual world around you, open your mind to experiencing the depths of your internal environment.

7. Sitting quietly or lying down, empty your mind of unhappy thoughts—anger, irritation, resentment, disappointment—and change to a positive outlook. Concentrate on being positive!

8. Think of yourself as a rag doll and collapse your body. Practice completely loosening every muscle you have.

9. Relax your mouth, lips, tongue, and throat. This is one method of turning off the constant words we turn over in our minds.

10. Practice releasing the muscles in the different areas of your face—cheeks, temples, lips, chin. Your face should be blank of all expression.

Techniques for handling stress

Many stressful situations may confront us during our normal daily tasks. Here are a few techniques for handling such situations.

1. Learn mental priority. Become aware of how rapidly and continuously your mind operates throughout the day. Periodically examine your thoughts, learning to sort out that which is worthwhile and that which is a waste of mental energy. Eliminate thoughts which are unnecessary and don't dwell on situations you can't change.

2. Develop your own plans for handling hectic situations when they occur. Practice these and your reactions to such situations will be controlled and relaxed.

3. When a bad situation does occur, resolve to handle it without emotion.

That will drain your energies. Take a deep breath, gather your thoughts, and make a businesslike effort at resolving it.

4. When you are the busiest, take a few moments to relax your thoughts and control preoccupation with your work. A brief retreat to a favorite spot or a quiet corner will keep tension under control and ultimately help you master your time.

In addition, recreational forms of physical and social activity offer an enjoyable release. The list of possibilities is endless—learn to play tennis or golf, take a walk or a hike, try sailing or skin diving, enroll in yoga class. Explore the possibilities and enjoy the pleasure—you've got a life to live!

There is a wealth of information available to help you master your time and your mind. The following books and articles are recommended as aids to your personal growth and mental well-being.

Suggested Readings

Books

Bahm, Archie J., *Yoga for Business Executives and Professional People*, New York: Citadel, 1965.

Curtis, J., and Detert, R., *How to Relax*, Palo Alto, Calif.: Mayfield, 1981.

Hill, Napoleon, *You Can Work Your Own Miracles*, Greenwich, Connecticut: Fawcett, 1971.

Hittleman, Richard, *Richard Hittleman's Guide to Yoga Meditation*, New York: Grosset and Dunlap, 1969.

Maltz, Maxwell, *Psycho-cybernetics and Self-Fulfillment*, New York: Grosset and Dunlap, (Bantam) 1970.

Peale, Norman Vincent, *Stay Alive All Your Life*, Greenwich, Connecticut: Fawcett, 1957.

Peale, Norman Vincent, *The Power of Positive Thinking*, New York: Prentice-Hall, 1952.

Peterson, Wilfred A., *The Art of Living, Day By Day*, New York: Simon and Schuster, 1972.

Stevenson, George S., *Master Your Tensions and Enjoy Living Again*, Englewood Cliffs: Prentice-Hall, 1959.

Articles

Collier, James Lincoln, "Leisure—Why Don't We Enjoy It More?" *Reader's Digest*, July 1973.

Knight, Leavitt A., Jr., "How to Relax Without Pills," *Reader's Digest*, February 1971.

Ratcliff, J. D., "How to Avoid Harmful Stress," *Reader's Digest*, July 1970.

Notes

1 Kenneth Pelletier, "Mind as Healer, Mind as Slayer," *Psychology Today*, February 1977, p. 33.

2 Hans Selye, "Forty Years of Stress Research," *California Medical Association Journal*, July 3, 1976, p. 55.

3 Frank Vitale, *Individualized Fitness Programs* (Englewood Cliffs, New Jersey: Prentice-Hall, 1973), p. 200.

"Ideal Figure" Weight Chart

A word about weight charts   Naturally, when you consult a height and weight chart, you assume it will tell you the appropriate weight for your height and bone structure. Before you accept a chart's "figures" as a guideline, however, you should be aware of the origin and significance of the statistics.

Unfortunately, most weight charts are based not on "ideal figures" but on statistical averages for a certain segment of the population. For example, the height and weight charts most commonly in use today are based on statistics compiled in 1959 by several insurance companies.[1] The records of these companies had shown that while an overweight person was a poor mortality risk, individuals who maintained their weight from age twenty-five on — whatever that weight might have been — had a lower death rate. Thus, the *average* height-weight figures for twenty-five-year-old men and twenty-five-year-old women as calculated on the basis of statistics provided by several million policy-holders, were deemed "desirable." The haphazard method of arriving at these averages has been pointed out by Ronald Deutsch: "The authors of the charts assumed men's clothes to weigh from seven to nine pounds and women's from four to six. They allowed two inches for women's shoes and one inch for men's. The result was an average of the inaccurate weights and heights of people in three different body styles, with the builds judged by standards which scientists have pronounced of extremely limited significance. Ignored completely was the fact that a great number of the subjects were too fat, possibly a third of them markedly so."[2]

Thus, even though your weight matches the weight recommended for you by most charts, you may well have to lose a few pounds more to obtain the figure you want. This "ideal figure" weight chart was designed on the basis of the figures of fashion models, airline stewardesses, and — most importantly — the thousands of men and women with whom the authors have worked over the past twelve years. On the basis of that experience, the weight indicated on this chart for your height and body frame is likely to be very close to the weight at which you will achieve the figure you desire. As you look at this chart, remember that most weight charts in general use today are not based on slim-figure averages, but rather on the statistical averages for a whole generation of "fat Americans!"

How to use the chart   To determine your frame size, take your wrist measurement. (This is just a rule-of-thumb measure; it will not be accurate in all cases, so use your judgment as well.) Measure circumference just above the wrist bone (toward the elbow) on the arm that you least use.

Small Frame:	4½" to 5⅛"
Medium Frame:	5⅜" to 6⅛"
Large Frame:	6¼" to 6¾"

Next, measure your height accurately. If you fall between two heights shown, add one pound for each quarter inch. For example, if you are medium frame, 5'6½" tall, your ideal weight would be 122 pounds. In order to find your ideal weight range, add five pounds above and five pounds below your ideal weight as determined from the chart, so the weight range for the woman described above would be 117 to 127 pounds. You should always attempt to stay within your weight range. There are always a few exceptions to any standard. You might find that you must go five pounds or so above or below your range to achieve the results you desire.

Remember that most weight charts in general use today are not based on slim-figure averages but rather on the statistical averages for a whole generation of "fat Americans." Also keep in mind that if you engage in strenuous activity such as weight training, you might tend to be slightly more heavy and still be within *your* ideal weight range. Weight is, after all, individual. When the image you see in the mirror is pleasing to you, you have achieved the figure you want.

Height	Small Frame	Medium Frame	Large Frame
4' 8"	65 lbs.	70 lbs.	75 lbs.
4' 9"	70	75	80
4' 10"	75	80	85
4' 11"	80	85	90
5' 0"	85	90	95
5' 1"	90	95	100
5' 2"	95	100	105
5' 3"	100	105	110
5' 4"	105	110	115
5' 5"	110	115	120
5' 6"	115	120	125
5' 7"	120	125	130
5' 8"	125	130	135
5' 9"	130	135	140
5' 10"	135	140	145
5' 11"	140	145	150
6' 0"	145	150	155
6' 1"	150	155	160
6' 2"	155	160	165

Notes

1 The following references contain a more detailed background of the weight charts from which this information was condensed:

Deutsch, Ronald M. *The Family Guide to Better Food and Better Health*. Des Moines, Iowa: Meredith (Better Homes and Gardens Creative Home Library), 1971.

Mayer, Jean. *Overweight: Causes, Cost, and Control*. Englewood Cliffs, N.J.: Prentice-Hall, 1968.

Solomon, Neil. *The Truth About Weight Control*. New York: Stein and Day, 1971.

Stuart, Richard B., and Davis, Barbara. *Slim Chance in a Fat World*. Champaign, Ill.: Research Press, 1972.

2 Deutsch, *Family Guide to Better Food . . .*, p. 122.

APPENDIX B

Energy Expenditure for Various Activities[1]

The values listed represent an average based on various representative groups of individuals. *Use them as an approximate figure.* To arrive at your expenditure of calories per minute, multiply the value opposite each activity or group of activities times your body weight. Then multiply that result times the number of minutes you spent in activity. The result will be your energy expenditure for that period of time. Each value, in other words, represents the number of calories used per pound each minute for the various activities.

Note

1 *Energy expenditure chart adapted from Clara Mae Taylor, Food Values in Shares and Weights* (New York: Macmillan, 1959), p. 12; C. F. Consolazio, R. R. Johnson and I. J. Pecora, *Physiological Measurements of Metabolic Functions in Man* (New York: McGraw-Hill, 1963), pp. 330–32; and, Phillip E. Allesen, Joyce M. Harrison and Barbara Vance, *Fitness for Life* (Dubuque: W. C. Brown, 1980), pp. 137–41.

Activity	Value
Sleeping	0.008
Sitting (includes eating)	0.010
Typing at an electric typewriter	0.012
Typing at a manual typewriter	0.014
Driving an automobile	0.015
Standing	0.016
Taking a bath or getting dressed	0.017
Cooking	0.021
House painting and walking (2mph)	0.023
House cleaning	0.025
Baseball, softball, and slow dancing	0.031
Bicycling (5.5mph), fencing and football	0.033
Archery	0.034
Golf	0.036
Badminton and volleyball	0.037
Swimming (2.5mph)	0.040
Boxing, walking downstairs, and level walking (4.5mph)	0.044
Basketball, table tennis, vigorous dancing, tennis, and horseback riding (trot or faster)	0.046
Water skiing and weight training	0.052
Soccer	0.060
Vigorous gardening	0.062
Handball	0.065
Racquetball	0.066
Vigorous skating	0.068
Squash	0.069
Mountain climbing	0.070
Jogging (5.5mph) and bicycling (13mph)	0.071
Skiing (5mph)	0.077
Vigorous calisthenics	0.097
Running (9mph)	0.103
Walking upstairs	0.116
Stationary running (140 counts per minute) and jumping rope at about same speed	0.162

Common Sources of Vitamins and Minerals

Common sources, functions, deficiency symptoms, and recommended daily allowances for fat- and water-soluble vitamins and major and trace minerals are listed in the tables on the following pages.

Fat-soluble vitamins

Vitamin	Sources	Function	Deficiency Symptoms	(RDA) Recommended Daily Allowance
A	Liver, fish liver oil, whole milk and cheese, cream, butter, fortified margarine, egg yolk, dark green leafy vegetables, deep yellow vegetables and fruits such as carrots, sweet potatoes, pumpkin, winter squash, apricots, peaches, and cantaloupe.	Essential for normal growth and maintenance of epithelial tissue and vision. Assists normal bone development and tooth formation, healthy sex glands, uterus and the linings of the bladder and urinary passages.	Night blindness, poor overall vision, skin and respiratory infections, dry scaly skin, abnormal bone and tooth enamel development, and reproductive disorders.	4000–5000 IU or 800–1000 RE for adults. 2000–3300 IU or 400–700 RE for children to 11 years of age. Excessive amounts may be toxic to children.
D	Exposure to sunlight, vitamin D milk, fortified foods, some in liver, egg yolk, tuna fish, salmon, and sardines.	Essential for normal growth and development and normal formation of teeth and bones. Assists absorption and metabolism of calcium and phosphorus. Aids prevention of osteomalacia and rickets.	Bone diseases such as rickets and osteomalacia, poor growth, and abnormal development of bones and teeth.	400 IU for children, pregnant, and lactating women. Otherwise sunlight and normal diet will insure an adequate amount. Amounts in excess of 1800 IU may be toxic to children.
E	Vegetable oils, shortening and margarine, whole-grain cereals, legumes, nuts, and dark green vegetables.	An antioxidant which prevents the oxidation of vitamin A in the intestinal tract, thus enabling it to be utilized; reduces the oxidation of fatty acids, protects red blood cells, plays a role in reproduction.	Possible muscular weakness, increased hemolysis of red blood cells, and macrocytic anemia. Defective infant absorption of fats and fat-soluble vitamins.	12–15 IU.

Vitamin	Sources	Function	Deficiency Symptoms	(RDA) Recommended Daily Allowance
K	Liver, vegetable oils (especially soybean), green leafy vegetables, cauliflower, tomatoes, cabbage and wheat bran.	Aids prothrombin production, which is necessary for blood clotting.	Delayed blood clotting and coagulation time. Possible internal bleeding.	RDA not established. Oral dose of 1–2 mg thought to be adequate for healthy persons. Toxic in large amounts.

Water-soluble vitamins

Vitamin	Sources	Function	Deficiency Symptoms	(RDA) Recommended Daily Allowance
C Ascorbic Acid	Citrus and other raw fruits and vegetables (especially the Puerto Rican cherry), melons, peppers, potatoes, and cabbage.	Essential for building collagen and providing firm tissues, strong blood vessels, tooth formation, bone formation and growth. Enhances absorption of iron, prevents scurvy, and related to biosynthesis of steriod hormones.	Scurvy, sore mouth, stiff aching joints, weak blood vessels, lassitude, impaired wound healing, and improper bone, cartilage, and tooth development.	45 mg
B₁ Thiamin	Meat (especially pork, liver and other organ meats), whole grain and enriched cereals, legumes (especially soybean), potatoes, nuts, and peanut butter.	Aids in the metabolism of carbohydrates. Prevents beriberi. Essential for growth, nervous system, digestion, normal appetite.	Beriberi, fatigue, anorexia, constipation, depression, irritability, abnormal carbohydrate metabolism.	0.5 mg per 1000 calories. Older adults need 1.0 mg.

	Sources	Functions	Deficiency Symptoms	Requirement
B₂ Riboflavin	Milk, dairy foods, organ meats, dark green leafy vegetables, eggs, enriched cereals, and breads.	Essential for healthy skin and vision in bright light. Prevents fissures at corners of mouth, around nose and ears, eye irritation and photophobia. Necessary in the breakdown of glucose to form energy.	Burning and itching eyes, blurred and dim vision, photophobia (eyes sensitive to light), inflammation of the lips and tongue, fissures in the corners of the mouth, nose and ears, greasy and scaly skin, digestive disturbances.	0.6 mg per 1000 calories. Somewhat higher for children and pregnant and lactating women.
Niacin	Fish, meat (especially organ), eggs, dark green leafy vegetables, whole grain and enriched breads and cereals.	Required for metabolism of carbohydrate, essential for healthy skin, normal function of the gastrointestinal tract, and nervous system; prevents pellagra.	Pellagra, nervous depression, neuritis, digestive problems, anorexia, and weakness.	13–18 mg.
B₆ Pyridoxine Pyridoxal Pyridoxamine	Pork and glandular meats, whole-grain breads and cereals, soybeans and other legumes, peanuts, oatmeal, milk, and eggs.	Needed for protein metabolism and the production of antibodies; aids niacin; prevents hypochromic anemia, seborrheic dermatitis, mucous membrane lesions. Essential for growth.	Neurologic problems, reduced growth rate in infants, nervous irritability, anemia, and anorexia.	2.0 mg.
B₁₂ Cyanocobalamin	Milk, eggs, cheese, liver, kidney, fish, and poultry.	Essential for the formation of normal red blood cells, the synthesis of protein, and the metabolism of nervous tissue. Related to certain anemias and to growth.	Sore tongue, signs of degeneration of the spinal cord, macrocytic anemia, poor appetite, poor coordination, and gastrointestinal disturbances.	3 mg for adults; 0.5–1.5 mg for infants; 2–3 mg for children; 4 mg for pregnant or lactating women.

Minerals	Sources	Function	Deficiency Symptoms	(RDA) Recommended Daily Allowance
Pantothenic Acid	Liver, eggs, kidney, fish (especially salmon), and yeast. Present in all plant and animal foods but the above are the best sources.	Essential for the breakdown of carbohydrates and fats. Involved in the synthesis of protein.	Irritability, restlessness, easy fatigue, and muscle cramps.	4–7 mg.
Folacin	Leafy-green vegetables, organ meats, poultry, fish, and whole grain cereals.	Required for the formation of DNA and normal maturation of red blood cells. Involved in the metabolism of protein and fats.	Toxemia of pregnancy and anemia, retarded production of white blood cells.	400 mg for adults; 100–300 mg for children.
Biotin	Liver, mushrooms, peanuts, yeast, milk and dairy products, egg yolk, bananas, grapefruit, tomato, watermelon, strawberries, and most vegetables.	Required in the metabolism of carbohydrates, fats, and amino acids.	Dermatitis (such as scaling), loss of appetite, nausea, muscle pains, high cholesterol levels.	100–200 mcg.

The data for both vitamin charts was adapted from Phyllis Sullivan Howe, *Basic Nutrition in Health and Disease* (Philadelphia: W. B. Saunders, 1976), pp. 87–108; Frank I. Katch and William D. McArdle, *Nutrition, Weight Control and Exercise* (Boston: Houghton Mifflin, 1977), pp. 22–27; Marie V. Krause and L. Kathleen Mahan, *Food, Nutrition and Diet Therapy* (Philadelphia: W. B. Saunders, 1979), pp. 177–180; Corinne H. Robinson, *Basic Nutrition and Diet Therapy* (New York: Macmillan, 1980), pp. 103–121.

Macronutrient* (major) minerals

Minerals	Sources	Function	Deficiency Symptoms	(RDA) Recommended Daily Allowance
Calcium	Milk and dairy products, greens (especially mustard, kale, turnip, collard), broccoli, cauliflower, clams, oysters, shrimp, salmon, and molasses.	Essential for normal growth of bones and teeth, transport of fluids across cell membranes, normal heart rhythm, muscle relaxation, and blood clotting. Maintains collagen and is a cofactor for several enzymes.	Bowed legs, growth retardation, and skeletal abnormalities (rickets), fragile and porous bones, poor tooth formation.	800 mg for adults; 800 mg for children; 1200 mg for teens; 350–550 mg for infants; 1200 mg for pregnant and lactating women.
Phosphorus	All protein-rich foods such as milk, eggs, cheese, meat, fish and poultry, whole-grain cereals, nuts, and legumes.	Associates with calcium in formation of bones and teeth. Aids the metabolism of fats and carbohydrates and in cell permeability. An energy carrier and a genetic enzyme. A part of every cell.	Rickets, osteoporosis (porous bones), osteomalacia (fragile bones), poor tooth formation.	Same as calcium except infants need from 200 to 400 mg.
Potassium	Whole grains, meat, legumes, fish and poultry, fruits, and vegetables.	Assists carbohydrate metabolism, conduction of nerve impulses, muscle contraction, regular heart rhythm, and synthesis of protein and is a component of intracellular fluid.	Apathy, muscular weakness, tachycardia, respiratory muscle failure, poor gastrointestinal tone; is associated with diabetes and kidney disease.	2500 mg.

Minerals	Sources	Function	Deficiency Symptoms	(RDA) Recommended Daily Allowance
Sodium	Table salt, seafood, meat, baking soda and powder, milk, and dairy foods. In most foods except fruit.	Regulates body fluid and osmotic pressure, water balance, muscle contraction, and nerve irritability.	Nausea, diarrhea, abdominal cramps, muscle cramps.	Same as potassium.
Magnesium	Whole grain cereals, legumes, nuts, milk, meat, leafy green vegetables.	A constituent of bones and teeth. Aids carbohydrate metabolism. Related to muscle and nerve irritability.	Malabsorption, loss of body fluids, tremor; is associated with alcoholism and severe renal disease.	350 mg for adults; 450 mg for pregnant or lactating women; 150–250 mg for children; 60–70 for infants.
Chlorine	Table salt, salty food, seafood, meat, and eggs.	Constituent of gastric juice; functions in conjunction with sodium, present in extracellular fluid. Serves as a buffer and an enzyme activator.	Prolonged vomiting, drainage from fistula, diarrhea.	2500 mg.
Sulfur	Protein-rich foods, nuts, and legumes.	Constituent of protein, a coenzyme; is needed for synthesis of essential metabolites.	Related to protein deficiency	No limit set. No deficiency has ever been observed in the United States.

Micronutrient* (trace) minerals

Minerals	Sources	Function	Deficiency Symptoms	(RDA) Recommended Daily Allowance
Iron	Liver, meat, egg yolk, kidney, poultry, prunes, peaches, apricots, raisins, dark green vegetables, legumes, whole-grain and enriched cereals, and molasses.	Constituent of hemoglobin and, as such, aids oxygen transfer; component of myoglobin in muscle.	Anemia, pallor, weight loss, fatigue weakness, and retarded growth.	10 mg for adults, infants, and children; 18 mg for teenagers and pregnant and lactating women.
Zinc	Liver and other organ meats, fish, wheat germ, yeast, and milk. Plant foods generally low.	Present in most tissues with higher amounts in liver, voluntary muscle, and bone. Constituent of many enzymes and insulin.	Seen only in severe malnutrition. Not seen in United States.	10 mg for adults and children; 15 mg for teenagers; 20 mg during pregnancy; 25 mg. during lactation; 3–5 mg for infants.
Iodine	Iodized table salt, seafoods, water, and vegetables.	Constituent of thyroxine and related compounds. Aids energy metabolism.	Goiter and mental retardation in infants.	130 mcg for adults; 115–150 mcg for teenagers and pregnant or lactating women. 60–110 mcg for children and 35–40 mcg for infants.
Fluorine	Fluoridated water, soybeans, spinach, gelatin, onions, lettuce.	May minimize bone loss. Reduces dental caries.	Dental caries and osteoporosis.	Not established.

Minerals	Sources	Function	Deficiency Symptoms	(RDA) Recommended Daily Allowance
Copper	Liver, shellfish, meats, nuts, legumes, whole-grain cereals, cherries, chocolate, poultry, and oysters.	Aids absorption and use of iron in synthesis of hemoglobin. Aids the metabolism of ascorbic acid and red blood cell formation and is a part of many enzymes.	No evidence of deficiency available.	Not established.
Manganese	Legumes, nuts, whole-grain cereals, beet greens, and blueberries.	Involved in the activization of many enzymes, the oxidation of carbohy-drates, the formation of urea, and protein hydroly-sis as well as bone growth.	No evidence.	Not established.
Selenium	Grains, onions, meats, milk, and various vegetables.	Aids fat metabolism and is an antioxidant.	Not known in human beings.	Not established.
Molyb-denum	Legumes, cereals, grains, organ meats, greens, and leafy green vegetables.	Not known in humans.	Not established.	
Chromium	Liver, corn oil, clams, whole-grain breads and cereals, cheese, and sometimes drinking water.	Essential for glucose metabolism and protein synthesis.	Found only in severe malnutrition, diabetes, and cardiovascular disease.	Not established.

*Dietary deficiencies in minerals are not likely to occur in the United States except for calcium and iron.

Both charts were adapted from Marie V. Krause and L. Kathleen Mahan, *Food, Nutrition and Diet Therapy* (Philadelphia: W. B. Saunders, 1979), pp. 125–128; Corrine H. Robinson and Marilyn R. Lawler, *Normal and Therapeutic Nutrition* (New York: Macmillan, 1977), pp. 141–145; Corrine H. Robinson, *Basic Nutrition and Diet Therapy* (New York: Macmillan, 1980), pp. 97–98; Eleanor Noss Whitney and Eva May Nunnelley Hamilton, *Understanding Nutrition* (St. Paul: West, 1977), pp. 381, 411.